# FAITH CRUSHED IN THE CLASSROOM:

## COMBATTING LIES
## AND EQUIPPING STUDENTS

## BY DANIELLA ORDONEZ

Faith Crushed in the Classroom

Trilogy Christian Publishers A Wholly Owned Subsidary of Trinity Broadcasting Network

2442 Michelle Drive Tustin, CA 92780

Rights Department, 2442 Michelle Drive, Tustin, CA 92780.

Trilogy Christian Publishing/TBN and colophon are trademarks of Trinity Broadcasting Network.

Cover design by: Grant Swank

For information about special discounts for bulk purchases, please contact Trilogy Christian Publishing.

Trilogy Disclaimer: The views and content expressed in this book are those of the author and may not necessarily reflect the views and doctrine of Trilogy Christian Publishing or the Trinity Broadcasting Network.

Manufactured in the United States of America

10 9 8 7 6 5 4 3 2 1

Library of Congress Cataloging-in-Publication Data is available.

ISBN: 978-1-68556-871-9

E-ISBN: 978-1-68556-872-6

## Special Thanks & Dedication

This book is in dedication to all of the students who are struggling to find themselves. The students who are faced with difficult decisions. The students who see a world of pain and are confused by all of the contradictory solutions. The students who just want to do what is right. This is for you.

This book is dedicated to my son, Jacob. I want to encourage you to ask questions and search for the answers. Remember that the Bible is your anchor for truth.

I want to thank Jesus for saving me when I didn't know how to save myself.

A special thanks to everyone who has supported me over the years.

Thank you to those of you who were patient with me through my discovery and later rejection of secular humanism.

# Table of Contents

# Preface

This book is the accumulation of experience, time, and prayer. The ideas represented in this book show the lens through which I have been able to more fully understand the world. The book weaves in and out of personal experiences and explanatory revelations. The book will, at times, read like a personal narrative and, at other times, may feel more academic in nature. The purpose of this is to reflect the very real way in which I was able to make sense of the circumstances I had faced. I am a researcher at heart, and circumstances such as that described in the book brought a lot of questions. The questions led to research, which led to even more questions. It wasn't until the missing puzzle piece was placed into the picture that I was able to more fully understand how all of the research would come together. As this book accumulates years of research and questions, it is nearly impossible to compile a resource list. Many of the statements made in this book are able to be easily validated through a simple internet search. I did provide the specific scriptures which supported my views from the Christian perspective, as this is most commonly misunderstood, and the answers to such viewpoints cannot be easily searched through the internet. All statements made in this book are designed to have you think more deeply about the common narrative we have learned through the shared teachings in the education system. I recognize that curriculum differs by state and focal points of specialized schools and/or college curriculums. My specific experience focuses on a very liberalized curriculum that some facets of such teachings have been implanted in nearly all education system ideologies and curriculums. I left the education system as a teacher in 2021. My testimony is based upon the internal and external struggles of faith as a college student. That is one layer of representation in this book. I also hold a post master's degree in secondary education, grades seven to twelve. I draw on my experiences as a teacher in New York through the lens of a Christian educator. Finally, as a mom, I offer a deep concern for little ones who are being exposed to this curriculum for over thirty-six hours per week with little to no parental framing. Parents need to have conversations with their students about the material they are learning to understand how this is being framed in their child's minds. I hope that this book will also speak to students who are struggling with their faith and equip them to powerfully take hold of both their faith and their education.

## Allow Me to Introduce Myself

Fear not, for I have redeemed you; I have called you by
your name; You are Mine.

Isaiah 43:1 (NKJV)

I was raised in an evangelical Christian home. I grew up going
to Sunday service and attending Bible studies during the week. I can
recall singing "Jesus Loves Me" and remember the emotional high
of youth retreats. I danced in church and took part in the Christmas
choir. I saw the Holy Spirit move powerfully through a congregation
as demons fled and elders prophesied boldly. I said my prayers each
night and told Jesus how much I loved Him. I made the decision to
be baptized at the tender age of nine years old because my pastor felt
that I was wise beyond my years. I gave Jesus my life and promised
to live each day for Him. At the time, I didn't fully know what that
meant. I simply knew that I had a purpose, that Jesus loved me, and
that I would figure it all out one day.

Childhood innocence faded as I entered my teen years. A time
with a great desire for acceptance, questions about the world, and a
lot of media programming. By the age of twenty-one, I had multiple
piercings, purple hair, a tattoo that says *coexist* (one of many), and
a really bad attitude. My outfit of choice includes fishnets, shorts, a
band shirt, a choker, and combat boots. Heavy metal is my music of
choice, weed is my escape, and God is a creation of humanity used to
control the population. How did I get here?

We all have our stories. Some of you are like me and have experienced rejection from peers, isolation, a single-parent home, and other child/teen traumas. In the name of love, security, and acceptance, my identity was slowly molded into whatever would meet those needs. I was sort of like a chameleon. I could be whatever you wanted me to be, as long as it meant I was given the attention and love that I craved. I mean, honestly, who didn't want to be like those beautiful celebrities on TV and the magazines? I believed that I had to look, talk, and act like them to be loved and accepted. The worst part was that Jesus wasn't cool. If you wanted to be in, He had to be out. I remember specifically being teased and called the "Jesus girl" or something to that effect. I found myself to be stuck. I wanted to fit into the world, but I also knew that angels were all around me and that God saw everything that I did. It was with this half-hearted faith and deep desire for acceptance that I made my way to college—as if middle and high school weren't traumatizing enough.

Win number one in college was the long-term relationship. I had always desired to have a boyfriend. I remember longing for love and relationship. I would tell myself, "I have so much love to give and nobody to give it to. Is something wrong with me?" For nineteen-year-old me, that's not a problem. I was physically in the best shape of my life and gained a lot of attention. I was loved, right? I had plenty of friends and would get invited to house parties. I was accepted. I was immensely busy with my theater group. I had a purpose. I worked and made pretty decent money as a server and bartender. I was secure. All of my deepest needs and desires were met, and I made it happen.

Why did I need God?

## A Faith-Crushing Experience

Truthfully, I didn't leave the faith right away. It was a process. God has blessed me with a logical mind. I love to learn about the facts, documentaries excite me, and I feel energized when my brain is working. At this point in my life, I was somewhere in between balancing the intellectual and the sublime. The mundane and profane always felt to be at odds with the heavenly and celestial. I was the girl who debated my atheist co-worker at the bar. I was the girl defending the faith to my satanist theater mate. I was the girl who challenged the professor after being bombarded with the teachings of agnostic philosophers. There was one particular moment that really shattered my fragile faith. It was my sophomore year of college. I walked into the third and last philosophy class that I had to take. I looked up at the board, and there it was, Nietzsche. "God is dead." "God is a human creation." "God is used to control the populace." I sat there slightly offended, but I wasn't yet ready to challenge my professor. He was a lot smarter than I was anyway, right? I mean, what could I possibly say? Aside from the fact that I learned what happened last time I made a comment in front of my peers which was in favor of a Christian worldview. That meant rejection. No, I couldn't go through that again. I sat there with my mind racing. I was fairly sure that God existed. I've had far too many supernatural experiences in my youth that were undeniable to not believe there was a spiritual world. I didn't personally know God; I just knew that His existence was far more likely than His non-existence.

I went home that night and contemplated all of these things. I found that in trying to understand how one would come to the conclusion that there is no God, I was beginning to understand my own doubts. Maybe my professor, who had claimed himself to be an atheist, had faith at one time in life. A little boy who prayed and heard silence. Maybe he saw the corruption of the televangelist, money in exchange for pardons, petitions, and prayers. Maybe he made one too many mistakes and was met with legalism, thus the importance of grace. In exchange for truth, he was sold the lie. God is dead. A swirl of black haze clouded my mind. I searched my personal library for something that could answer my questions. There it was, a little white book on science and the Bible. I thought that maybe someone else could say it better than I felt equipped to handle. I went in the next day and sat through another lecture about how our society has surpassed the need for an invented God. I took a deep breath, handed him the book, and waited. I approached him three days later, asking what he thought. He looked at the book, looked at the trash, and said, "This is garbage; throw it out." I was in shock. I felt the weight of a thousand bricks. This was only the beginning of the journey I would now embark on to lose and rediscover my faith. I say all of this looking back on the situation. They say hindsight is 20/20. Sometimes it takes confronting your fears, doubts, and critics to strengthen what you know to be true. "Veritas," said Pilate to Christ. Pilate, my professor, and I had something in common. We all needed John 14:6. Can you relate?

The thing is that it isn't only philosophy class that can lead to a faith crisis. It's other classes as well. My other classes were built around a very linear storyline. We were taught of holy wars waged in the name of Christianity. Centuries of bloodshed in the name of religion, money, and power. We were taught about early American Christians who hanged witches and owned slaves. We were taught that the age of imperialism was meant to spread Christianity. We were taught about the gods of the Greco-Roman empire. We were taught Egyptian mythology and learned about the afterlife. We were taught the theory of evolution and told that our existence was nothing more than mere chance. We were taught that humans were cancer to the earth, so we better recycle. We were taught about Muhammad, Buddha, and Krishna. We were taught to stand for what is right, but our moral compass was centered on our own personal thoughts and beliefs. For everything we were taught, there was so much that we did not learn. Excluded from our education was the message of the gospel. Excluded were the countless churches that fought against slavery and racism. Excluded were the missionaries who fed the poor. Excluded were the words of Jesus, who taught that not everyone who claimed to know Him was actually of Him. Excluded was the value of each human life as an intentional creation. Excluded was a more conservative moralistic worldview. Excluded were the many scientists, philosophers, and mathematicians who believed beyond a shadow of a doubt that there was a God. Excluded were the historical accounts of the persecution of the early church. The education system focuses heavily on inclusivity, and yet we were excluded. I sat through many lectures and heard the judgments made about Christians. In a traditional college setting, Christianity is often viewed as synonymous with Republican. The social engineering of the 2016 election really caused a great divide in our country and for this generation. This book is not meant to spark a political debate but rather to point your attention to the culture that has been created around the social discourse. We live in a society where if we don't like something, we cancel it. We delete, remove, and block. None of which is a healthy way to engage in debate. Would it surprise you to learn that the college classroom is not very different? I could recall countless examples of this type of thinking from professors, guest speakers, and peers.

So here was the Molotov cocktail of my senior year: low self-esteem, pain, an identity crisis, and wavering faith. I didn't graduate college prepared to fully embrace the world. Instead, I came out with more questions than I had in the first place. Some days I was an agnostic atheist. Other days a self-proclaimed spiritualist who ascribed to New Age and Jain teachings, which is really just witchcraft. Quite frankly, some of you reading this right now might not even see the problem with witchcraft as it has become so normalized in our generation. I will save that for a later chapter. It's safe to say I was really confused. I didn't know who I was, what I was meant to do, what to believe, or who was right. There was an empty void inside that seemed to grow larger every day. I know that there are many students out there who have felt or currently feel this way. I know there are many of you out there who feel like God has failed you, and what you're learning now feels truer or more tangible. I know that you picked up this book for a reason. You are not alone. This is for you.

# My Confusion

For God is not the author of confusion, but of peace.

1 Corinthians 14:33 (KJV)

Remember in chapter one I mentioned a tattoo I had? Well, that tattoo was inspired by a bumper sticker. You might have seen it before! The image shows different religious symbols and spells out the word "coexist." The secular education system fits perfectly with the coexist idea. This idea is simply a Segway into the New Age religion. As with all things, there is a reason why it is attractive. New Age or spirituality allows you to adopt the attitude of "I am spiritual, but not religious." If I had a dollar for every time I said that, well, you know how the saying goes. It gives you permission to live the college lifestyle of going to parties, drinking underage, and hooking up without any conviction or realization that what you're doing has very real consequences both in this life and eternity. It wasn't until I got married that I realized the impact that lifestyle had on my concept of love and intimacy. It allows you to be the moral compass of your own life. What is true for you may not be true for me, and neither way is wrong. It allows you to shift responsibility to karma and trust that we can work off the bad stuff later. This is yet another piece of the problem. To move away from a grounded concept of morality means a lot of grey space. Grey space is not necessarily a bad thing, but it sure is a poor indicator of moral correctness.

### New Age Religion

New Age is attractive to people who have rejected the idea of organized religion and all of the hypocrisy that seems to be bred within it. The church has lost so many youths to spirituality. What makes this dangerous is how closely it resembles faith. Jesus is no longer your Savior but an ascended master who was sent to lead the way. He is not the only ascended master; Krishna, Buddha, Muhammad, and others have also evolved into a state of perfected godhood. The New Age religion also teaches that you, too, are a god. You see, the serpent doesn't come up with new tricks; he just manipulates the same lies. In the same way that Eve was promised to be as God, this belief system teaches that you are divine and can tap into Christ consciousness. Sounds attractive so far.

At the time, I believed it was impossible for us to really know the answers. I did not believe there was a God in the way that we were taught. God was a metaphor for the universe. God was a force, and from this force came life: planets, stars, aliens, and humans. I believed in reincarnation. That our soul was constantly evolving, and we had unlimited chances to get it right until we attained godhood. I have to thank my dad, who asked me, "Well, how do you work off bad karma as an insect?" It's a good question. It was such a good question that it caused some serious doubt about my new beliefs! I began to pick up the teachings of Jainism, which is a religion that promotes peace through the practice of non-involvement. I believed in it so much that I left notes on bathroom walls leading people to these teachings so that they could be set free from the shackles of their minds.

The coexist movement is deceptive, and my college classroom primed me to accept its teaching. Even more disturbing is that the same issue described as social justice is being brought to younger grades each year. All of which is more priming to accept this system of belief. The movement sounds great to any person who sees a world of evil. Our history classes teach us about wars, oppression, violence, and hatred. Media outlets are constantly showing us worldwide atrocities. So, of course, my next natural question is, why does a God that loves allow such atrocities? Students are not being taught that God is the answer. These issues are constantly presented, God is evil for letting them happen, and so it is up to humanity to solve the problems. This is why you hear people say faith in humanity is either destroyed or restored. We learn that we are the agents of change, and praying to the non-existent God is a waste of time. We live in a world where faith is placed in humans who follow their own beliefs as to what is and is not morally correct. Humans are not without flaws. You cannot create a perfect society through the hands of imperfect people. I am sure you have asked these same questions, or at least know others who share these thoughts. I never shied away from the tough questions. My hope is to be able to answer some of those questions for you throughout the book.

## The New Age Appeal

Coexist is a founding principle of the New Age religion. The main idea is that all religions can unite together and live in peace and tolerance of one another. This includes the concept that no matter which path we take in life, we will reach the same place in the end. According to New Age belief, we all believe in the same god. It is important to understand why this movement is so attractive. Rather than write it off as one of the social ills of the millennial and Gen Z generations, we must seek to understand why people are drawn in by it. Let's dive a bit deeper into these concepts.

C is represented by the half-crescent moon with the star (Islam). There is a place in liberalized ideology that focuses on Islamophobia. This is defined as the irrational fear of Muslims. This sociological concept was born out of fear stemming from the attack on the Twin Towers on September 11, 2001. O is represented by the peace sign. Peace and love to all. Our world recounts countless wars and very few periods of peace. E is represented by the male and female symbols to signify gender equality. This piece is evident for both the modern feminist movement and LGBTQ groups. X is represented by the star of David, which connects to the Jewish nation. We learn about the atrocities that took place during World War 2 and historical accounts of antisemitism. I and S are represented with the wheel of dharma and the yin-yang. Buddhism and other Eastern esoteric philosophies have become very popular in recent years. The practice of yoga and meditation has spread throughout the Western world and is offered in schools, private studios, and the workplace. A practice that many do not realize has deeply rooted spiritual implications. T is represented by the cross of Christianity. I have read countless books and learned in history the role that Christianity has played in the world, according to the secular humanist curriculum. Unfortunately, mankind has used the name of Christianity for personal gain, and rarely have I heard stories of someone truly reflecting the nature of Christ. Throughout the whole coexist movement, there is an underlying belief at work. That belief is that all of these other religions are well-meaning, tolerant, and ultimately good. Christianity is the hateful, intolerant aggressor with a mission to proselytize the world. According to the worldview in which coexist is needed, all other religions are merely victims at the mercy of the hateful villainous Christians. Can you relate to having felt the weight of this narrative?

**Metrics to Measure Our World**

The narrative is appealing to anyone who has been taught about a world full of hatred. To the individual who wants to see freedom and liberation for the world. The problematic piece is that our view of the world is composed of our personal experiences, family upbringing, media influence, education, and so on. What is mostly encouraged is living from a place of our subjective reality. If we believe it to be true, then it must be so. Beliefs such as this position the self as the center of the world. All of what happens around me is filtered through the lens of my feelings. This is problematic because truth cannot be subjective. When I would teach my seventh-grade students the point of view in a text, I often used the example of different people standing around a statue in a museum. Each person stood looking at a different part of the statue, and if each were asked to describe what they saw, they would only have their portion to describe. This, however, does not indicate the full picture of the statue or the reality of the existence of its other pieces. Now imagine you read the description card, and it mentions that the statue was created a hundred years ago. You don't necessarily have evidence to prove that is true; in fact, from where you're standing, it looks less than ten years old, chiseled in pristine marble. Regardless of your point of view, the truth is that it's a hundred years old. It's kind of like this with God too.

Truth needs to be objective and detached from our feelings. Emotions are a very powerful thing. It is the key to connecting us with one another. Unfortunately, our emotions tend to be the driving force behind reality in this post-modernist world. We must come to terms with the fact that not everyone's truth can be objectively true. Albeit each individual's truth is very real to them, still making it a subjective reality. I firmly believe that if we could really just grasp the difference between subjective and objective reality, we would understand core societal issues at a much deeper level. You see, we live in a world of decisions made through subjectivity. Truth by definition consists of something based on fact or reality. One might say the weather feels like 103 degrees when, in fact, the thermometer reads 87 degrees. Does that mean it is truly 103 degrees just because somebody feels that it is? Of course not! Consider the metric you use to measure your world. Is truth at the center of your reality, or do you judge the world around you based on your subjective truth? There is a sentiment being tossed around to "live your truth" and to "go your own path," and in doing so, we will all arrive at the same place. If you open any GPS map, you'll see different roads. If each road represents a different belief system, you can see that these roads take you to different places. If we can look at a simple map and see that not all roads lead to the same place, what makes us think that the metaphor for our spiritual journey is any different?

# Defining the Problem

For all that is in the world—the lust of the flesh, the lust
of the eyes, and the pride of life—is not of the Father but
is of the world.

1 John 2:16 (NKJV)

It is very easy to adopt the beliefs constantly reinforced to us if
we are not firmly rooted in our faith in Christ. We will dive deeper
into the generally accepted system of beliefs masked as secular in later
chapters. This chapter serves to discuss some of the other influences
in our lives that confuse our identity, hinder our beliefs, and distract
us from the truth. In the search for answers and fulfillment, we can
be easily misled.

It is my firm belief that we feel a void because God wants us to
seek Him. God placed eternity in our hearts, and as a result, we ask
questions about our existence and search for the answers.[1] Mankind
is unique in that we question things, such as where we will go when
we die? Without the concept of eternity, it would not be within our
human nature to ask such questions. The world systems have been
designed to answer those questions for you, which normally result in
working off bad deeds and relying on yourself. This is why the Christian
faith is unique. A true relationship with God does not ask you to clean
yourself up to be okay in God's eyes. There is accountability for our
actions that must be taken, as there are natural consequences for what
we do. However, God describes believers as His children. In times of
pain and trouble, His children may walk away from Him, but there is

no length that He will not go to draw you back to Himself. God desires a relationship with His creation. When we search for fulfillment in the world, we turn up empty and exhausted. This is why social media paints a dangerous picture. It creates a reality that is more deception than reality. It tells you all of the answers for acceptance, love, identity, and security relay in the systems of the world and the people who run them. I assure you, this is a lie. What may look like a happy social media post is often a mask for the broken individual using this means to escape the pain they feel inside. Only one person can truly fill that inner void. The Bible tells us if we search for God, we will find Him.[2] With this in mind, take heart in knowing that your questions and desires are not in vain. The world often has a temporary fix to whatever it is that seems to plague us. This is because we live in a world full of distractions and empty promises. A world of smoke and mirrors.

Subtle distractions move us further away from God and draw us closer to ourselves. The world is designed to keep us in this perpetual state of searching, finding temporary fulfillment, and burning out. When starting college, we are asked to make a huge life decision right then and there. We are asked to choose a major that is going to decide a course of study for the next four years that will determine a life-long career. The problem is that the average high school senior has no idea what they want to be, let alone truly know who they are. In the digital age that we live in, the answer is an internet search away. All you have to do is reach into your pocket and find a world of information. We chase after a life that we think will earn us the most clout. This means compromising ourselves, our values, what we think is right, and what we know is right for social brownie points. We are influenced by the influencers—when God has called us to be the ones doing the influencing for Him.

Cell phones serve to connect us with the world in a multitude of ways. One of the biggest influences in our lives is the media. We are plugged in (I mean this almost literally) to a world of convenience. New virtual reality spaces allow us to plug into alternate realities and fantasy worlds. Video games allow us to escape reality and live out those fantasies. The news is plastered all over the place with its message of fear, division, and media bias. We are constantly posting on social media, seeking the approval of others. Be honest, what do you do if a post doesn't get enough likes? You probably delete it. What if Rosa Parks decided to stay seated in the back of the bus because it wasn't the popular thing to do? The popular thing is not always the right thing. We need to understand that it is through these technological mediums that we believe we can be fed the solutions to all of our problems. Our phones have become an idol. Anything that we place before God in our lives is an idol. We consult it when we have questions, and we use it to express our feelings, connect with others, buy new things, and so much more. Now am I saying you shouldn't have a phone? Of course not! We do need to use our phones and social media responsibly, though. Just because something is at our fingertips doesn't mean that we should engage. Ask God to show you what responsible social media use looks like so that you can lead in changing the cultural climate.

Why am I spending so much time on this? It is key for the college student to unplug from these distractions and spend time with Jesus in order to maintain strength in the faith. I don't mean a five-minute prayer. I mean really taking time to seek His face in fellowship and guidance. The years spent in the school system bring great vulnerability. This is where your faith is either destroyed or strengthened. The school system is only one piece of the puzzle. So much of the current generation has been raised by technology. Parents must set the standard for technology use in their homes. Make time for the family without cell phones, laptops, and tablets. We are all plugged in and must learn how to unplug from distractions and plug into God. This is something that I truly believe to be a huge source of distraction today and an easy way to influence others as well as ourselves. Modern algorithms are designed in order to cater to our likes and filter out our dislikes. You will often see ads for things you agree with and not things that you don't, which can be dangerous to our spiritual condition. Our devices create a sort of subjective reality. For example, while I was in college and into the New Age beliefs, every advertisement and suggested video was based on these preferences. Now that I know Jesus Christ to be the truth, it was a scary thought that, without the grace of God, it would have been extremely difficult to find a sermon that would have spoken to my heart. The odds of coming across a video that would plant a seed of truth were slim to none, as it would not have met my search preferences. I do believe that God can influence anything, and so I encourage you to share a video when it glorifies God because you don't know who is watching and who might be impacted by it. Remember that eyes are the windows to the soul.

We must protect our eye gates and our ear gates. This means being wise in what we watch and what we hear. As a female, I can say (and I know young men experience this as well) that comparison is a big problem. When we constantly see what we don't have, we can begin to invite depression into our lives. Did you catch that? I used the word invite. Typically the things that enter our lives do so because we allow them. We give permission to these things by watching, listening, and agreeing with what is presented in front of us on a daily basis. If you find yourself constantly compelled to be connected to your phone, a technology fast may be in order. Cell phone and social media usage can be an addiction.

Not only are we in need of discernment about what we expose ourselves to on our devices, but we need to be asking God to filter the people in our lives. Our friends can easily influence our decisions. When we see them posting a bunch of pictures from the latest dorm party, the temptation to conform becomes much stronger. Ask God to bring you Christian friends that are going to uphold biblical values. We have been conditioned to believe that the college experience of partying, drinking, and missing class is normal because of the movies. So-called "college party culture" is empty and misleading. Hollywood has simply polluted your thinking concerning this time period. The truth is that it's an important time when we learn life-long values of responsibility, commitment, and growth. I know people that took seven years to graduate from a four-year program simply because of falling into party culture. I also know people who have passed away while in college, and so the whole "I want to live my party years and straighten up later" excuse won't work. We are never guaranteed tomorrow, and everyone thinks it won't be them.

This is a time of spiritual vulnerability. We must constantly check the condition of our hearts. It is from our hearts that all of our desires come forward. Ask yourself, what do I have to gain from engaging with these people and acting in these behaviors? There is always a payoff. More often than not, it is a deep need for acceptance and purpose. Aligning our hearts with God is the key to success. He will show you where your true acceptance lies. He will reveal to you the purpose of your life. How can He do that? Well, God created our world. He exists outside of time, and so He has seen the beginning and the end. This means He has seen your life and how it will play out. So instead of playing the guessing game, you can just ask Him. Only God knows the deepest places of our hearts, and we need His help during this crucial period of our lives.[3] Fortunately, if we stop looking to ourselves and the world for the answers, we will learn that God has the answers.[4] Reading this with the euphemism of "follow your heart" is now absolutely terrifying. If I am struggling with past hurts, a lack of fulfillment, and no life direction, I am surely going to end up anxious, depressed, angry, confused, or many other things. The fruit that I then bear is not going to be good if this is what is in my heart. The change can only come by the smallest seed of faith. In order to uproot what has planted itself into our hearts and minds, we must root ourselves in faith.[5] All it takes is faith the size of a mustard seed! We are told to live by faith, and in doing so, we will please God.[6]

We have discovered that there is a major struggle between the condition of our hearts and faith in God. We learned that we have a bit of an identity crisis. We don't know much about ourselves, even though we think we do, yet our hearts deceive us. We don't yet fully know or understand God, and as humans, we spend time filling our lives with meaningless things that lead to temporary fulfillment (the book of Ecclesiastes is all about this). We must realign our thinking about God's character, our identity, and how we turned our hearts away from Him in the first place. This problem is bigger than each individual. The next chapter will talk about purpose. The school system has a way of influencing and shaping the culture of each generation, and young people, in particular, are especially fertile ground. Our common spiritual enemy understands this, and this is why the school years are the most important years of our development.

## Fueled with Purpose

I know that You can do everything, And that no purpose of Yours can be withheld from You.

Job 42:2 (NKJV)

The purpose of a person's life is very often tied to identity in ways that are both beneficial and detrimental to our growth. There is a big push in the education system for social-emotional learning, and topics such as identity are usually present. The framing around identity and purpose is one that places humanity at the forefront of salvation and is often tied to what we are able to accomplish. We all have a unique set of talents and gifts that are meant to work together with the Holy Spirit for us to accomplish the special assignment(s) placed on our lives. We won't be able to walk in our purpose without a right understanding of God or a working knowledge of our identity in Him. This is another key area of attack from the enemy. Many people settle for comfortability and fail to accomplish their purpose. Many partake in the wide variety of distractions placed before us, which rob us of what God has for us. Each person has been given a heavenly assignment to accomplish. It takes time and pursuit to walk out that purpose. We cannot understand the fullness of the assignment we have been given if we do not spend time with God. Some of these distractions could be relationships, social media, and other pressures, both school and not school-related. That's not to say they are bad things, but without a proper balance, they can distract you from going deeper with God.

Social influences also play a big role. Can I let you in on a little secret? From middle school all the way up through college, the number of friends you will carry into adulthood slowly begins to decline. Sometimes, you drift apart as friends. And other times, life just happens. You'll go to different schools, get married, and start your careers. We think that our number one priority is our friends. While social experiences are important, our friends play a major role in either helping us walk toward our purpose or leading us away from it. Choose your friends wisely. When you connect with other people who are driven to succeed, have their priorities in line, and care about their spiritual life, then you are setting yourself up for excellence.

School years can be a really confusing time. Fortunately, the Bible gives us tools to be well equipped and able to handle life's challenges. As believers, we are told to put on the full armor of God[7] and head into battle. Every day is a battle. The enemy never stops. Why should we? Do you know what he loves the most? A lazy adolescent. Why? Because this is one of the most influential times of your life. If he can waste your youth, he can help set up bad habits that will be carried with you into adulthood. The enemy understands the power of young people. Samuel was called to do great things by the Lord at twelve years old. David was anointed at fifteen. Joseph began getting wild dreams from the Lord at seventeen. Esther became queen of Persia at around fourteen. These are only a few examples, and the truth is that it goes beyond age. Your brain is in the process of development. Every choice you make has either a negative or positive consequence. Our brain comes into full development at twenty-five years old. It becomes very difficult to change our thoughts and habits once these connections have been established. Save yourself the high cost of negative choices and start the process of mind renewal while your brain is still figuring things out.

**Bad Decisions and Wrong Thinking**

Do you not feel motivated to go to church or fellowship with other believers? Does church sound boring, and you feel dragged to go? Did I mention you are a prime target for spiritual warfare? Remember that thing I said earlier about putting on the armor of God? As mentioned above, God calls young people, and the enemy knows it. The enemy of our soul will lie to us about God, other believers, our parents, and even ourselves. Once the enemy can keep you away from other believers and those more mature in the faith, he can lie to you through negative thoughts. This is what he did to me. I stopped going to church. I was always too tired or not in the mood. I started hanging out with the wrong people. I started going to parties and drinking to numb the pain. What came as a result? My heart turned away from God. I had negative judgments about the believers in my life because I had been hurt by church people. The enemy used those things against me, and I began to search for the answers to my questions outside of God's Word. The enemy would also twist the Word of God and speak to me through a false perception I held because of the pain. I was angry at God, hated my parents, didn't feel accepted or good enough, and I was totally confused. Some of the questions I would ask were: If God knew all of this would happen, why create us? Why is God so hateful in the Old Testament? Isn't He a God of love? Why is sin such a big deal if everyone does it? If God loves us all, why would anybody go to hell? Why are Christians so unlike Jesus? And of course, God, do You even exist?

These are the questions that plagued me. These would lead to even deeper theological questions with no real understanding or ability to answer. There are several things that I can say led to my heart turning away from God, but nothing rings truer than Hosea 4:6 (NKJV), "My people are destroyed for lack of knowledge." We have young people wearing a mask on Sunday and changing the mask on Monday. Our identity is found solely in the one who created us. There are many who never come to this realization because of the brainwashing that occurs from a young age through the education system. A curriculum that leads to our faith being crushed in the classroom. We have been primed from a young age to deny the reality of God and His activity in our lives. If we don't know God, we can't know ourselves.

In light of this, I will say that we have a generation hungry for truth. A generation of young people that genuinely want to impact the world and stand for what is right. The next question to ask is, who is leading you? If you are not learning from the church, then we know you're learning from somewhere else. Maybe that is why you are reading this. Maybe you are reading this in search of answers. The purpose of this book is to bridge some of the gaps in our understanding of biblical truth when compared to the current education system's preference of thought, which is secular humanism. I hope to be able to answer some of those deep theological questions that had not been answered for me. I hope to help you understand the problem of sin, the wrath of God as justice, the love of God as grace, and your role as a believer.

## And They Were of One Mind

And the Lord said, "Indeed the people are one and they all have one language, and this is what they begin to do; now nothing that they propose to do will be withheld from them."

Genesis 11:6 (NKJV)

The public education system guides students into placing faith in themselves in order to contribute to the greater good of humanity. This is really the purpose laid out for them. As I am writing this, I can picture the humanist poster hanging on the wall in my old classroom. There were a number of kids holding hands, standing on the globe. Humanist thinking paints that sort of picture. That we must all do our part for the bettering of society, and this relies on tolerance, inclusivity, and social ethics, all at the expense of others. The end justifies the means type of thinking. One particular way of thinking which is broadly applied is called situational ethics. As long as something is done for the greater good of society, it is acceptable and can be applied in our world. This means removing our right to free speech, surrendering privacy rights, and the acceptance of protection laws that we do not support.

### John Dewey and Collective Thought

An influential signee of the Humanist Manifesto was a man named John Dewey. His theories around education paved the way to change the American school system forever. John Dewey of Columbia University is celebrated as one of the best-known academics, philosophers, and public intellectuals. Dewey supported something known as collective thought or collective learning. He did not believe in God's existence, but he believed in preserving religious practice. He believed in joining together in community to focus on ideals and take positive action together. According to Dewey, community, ideals, and striving to be our best were God.

Collective thought refers to an unspoken agreed-upon set of beliefs. Differing thoughts, if believed to stem from faith in God, are often disregarded, silenced, and even punished. This plays itself out in the classroom more often than you'd think. A teacher is taught that they must remain unbiased. Truthfully, many teachers are humanists themselves, and in an effort to create an emotionally safe classroom environment, the mention of anything God-related is shut down pretty quickly. This means that there really isn't a healthy debate taking place. While I was in college, I remember having a certain view about a specific issue. My opinion was contrary to what may have been considered the popular opinion. You would think that there would be an open discussion in an effort to prove or disprove the statement that I made. The response of the classroom was quite different. Several students perked up, sounding offended at what I had said. They created their own assumptions and nearly jumped down my throat. One girl, in particular, threw a fit and never spoke to me again. That's only one experience.

Let me give you another example of a similar situation. There was a woman who was studying psychology. Christianity, as well as other belief systems, hold the view that demonic entities can, in some cases, be responsible for mental illness. There is a story where a man spent his life isolated, crying and cutting himself with stones as a result of demonic possession (Mark 5:1–20). I know many Christians who have been set free from the chains of insanity, bipolar disorder, depression, anxiety, panic disorder, schizophrenia, and more. I personally can testify to this change. I was set free from depression, panic, and anxiety only through the Holy Spirit in 2018. There are, in fact, real stories of people being set free from these oppressive forces in the name of Jesus. The young woman who was taking the psychology class held true to this belief. Her professor made a comment along the lines of, "Some people actually believe that demons cause these types of behaviors." The young woman, staying true to what she believes, responded by saying that she does believe that can, in fact, be the case. The young woman recalls the professor and her classmates looking down on her from then on and, in her own words, "Treating me as if I was something stuck to the bottom of their shoe." The popular opinion was so against what she believed that her opinion was shunned and thrown away as a myth. She was also completely humiliated. This type of attitude in the classroom disregards the testimony of many people, including my own, as fiction. Collective thought destroys the individual while claiming that the individual is celebrated. It denies our personal values and rejects our experiences as individuals for the sake of creating a seemingly better and more unified society.

**One Body, One Spirit**

I love the arts. There is something beautiful about being able to express the fullness of human emotion onto a canvas, a screen, music, or words. I believe this is one of the many gifts that God gives us because He is the ultimate artist. Look at the beauty of nature or the intricacies of a human cell. It is nothing short of beautiful and precise. The human body reflects the complexity and beauty of the handiwork of God. Different parts work together for the functioning of a human being. The same is true in the body of Christ. We all represent a part of the body and have been designed to perform its function. Just like a physical body, all are joined together, receiving commands from the head (the brain). The body has to be of one mind in order for it to function to its full capacity. Collectivism and interdependence, at its core, are intended to be performed under the headship of Christ. There is great power in like-mindedness. Part of this idea of collectivism is to have many people of like-mind because, in the spirit, there are very real manifestations of the supernatural. This is like when a Christian believes that when believers come together, the Spirit of God is made manifest on the earth. This means that when many believers come together and are of the same mind, the presence of God becomes so strong and very powerful. This idea applies to non-believers as well. The enemy works hard to create a narrative that is anti-Christ, and when others come into agreement with the lies about the one and only true God of the universe, then the spirit manifested in its fullness is of the antichrist spirit. Atheistic humanism, at its core, is developing the like-mindedness needed for the body of non-believers to make manifest the spirit of the antichrist on the earth. This can come forward through various mediums. I will give you an example of one specific medium that I have experienced firsthand.

In college, I was a standing member of the executive board for the school's theater organization. Not only was I involved in leadership, but I also produced, directed, and acted in various productions. I had to take on different roles and imagine myself in the position of other people. I realize now that I had opened myself up to some pretty crazy demonic influences. This can happen when you are not covered spiritually. In fact, there are many well-known celebrities who claim that when they are performing, something else takes over. I remember one year, I was working for a haunted house and was playing three different roles in two upcoming shows. The method for getting into character involved acting as the character without breaking. This is the same type of method of acting that Heath Ledger (the actor that played the Joker in the *Dark Knight*) also practiced. The details surrounding his death, which took place a few short months after filming, were mysterious, to say the least. They found a diary with some pretty scary in-character writings. The extended periods of isolation and character experimentation led to insanity. In his own words to *Empire Magazine* in 2007, Ledger states,

> I sat around in a hotel room in London for about a month, locked myself away, formed a little diary and experimented with voices – it was important to try to find a somewhat iconic voice and laugh. I ended up

landing more in the realm of a psychopath – someone with very little to no conscience towards his acts. He's just an absolute sociopath, a cold-blooded, mass-murdering clown.[8]

It isn't hard to manifest a spirit of murder when coming into an agreement through the method of acting that you are trying to portray. In my own experience, there was one point when I didn't even know who I was. I felt so lost and began taking on the characteristics of all of these other people.

Why am I telling you this story? Studying the humanities asks us to do the same. It asks us to step into the shoes of other people and to try to understand their point of view. This can be a good thing; it can produce compassion for others. However, we need to be firmly planted in the Word of God in order to understand more about their condition. Why did they do the things they did? Why did they view the world the way they did? What happened in their lives? When learning about these subjects, you will often read a biography of the artist, author, or philosopher. It's the age-old euphemism that is present. Does life inspire art, or does art inspire life? I say it is a bit of both.

## The Manifestation of the Manifesto

The fool has said in his heart, "There is no God."

Psalm 14:1 NKJV

The Humanist Manifesto was signed by both religious and secular humanists. The first manifesto was signed in 1933, the second in 1973, and the third in 2003. The American Humanist Association's tagline and aims encompass clearly what they believe. Their tagline reads, "good without a God." The aim of the association is to advocate progressive values and equality for humanists, atheists, and freethinkers. What are some of these progressive values? When we dig a little deeper, you would be surprised to know that these values have greatly impacted the way that the population views the world. We will explore eight key pieces to the Humanist Manifesto.

**Humanist Belief #1: The universe is self-existing and not created.**

It is incredible to me how the world can be in perfect balance to support life, and yet those who hold this belief chalk it up to mere chance. In fact, science really just serves to study what is already in existence. To use science to try to answer the creation question is futile. It is very difficult to say with certainty when exactly something was created. Common scientific methods used to measure the time that the world has existed are not without error. Science and faith don't have to disagree. In fact, science explains what currently is in existence and only further confirms an intelligent creator. This does not include pseudo-scientific theories which have been glorified as fact rather than theory. It is impossible to actually measure the theories of macro-evolution (one being becoming another) and the age of the earth as millions of years old. The scientific method includes actually being able to measure the means by which you test your hypothesis. It is impossible to do that when it comes to these areas.

My husband is a big fan of watching those shows where the animals are themselves in their natural habitat. We watch and look at the beauty, variety, and complexity of each living being. We marvel when we see the breathtaking mountains or the precision of symmetry in flowers and plants. How can any of that be an accident of nature? Chaos cannot create order in and of itself. Chaos creates chaos. You don't smash a bunch of car parts together and hope for a fully functioning vehicle. In fact, the car parts would have had to have existed to be smashed together in the first place. An intelligent being must be present in placing together the parts. We often hold God to the same rules of time and space that we abide by. The problem with this is that God exists outside of time. It's sort of like a video game. The game has an intelligent creator in order to make the world of the game come together. The player even has influence over the actions that take place within the game. The creator exists outside of the game and is therefore not held to the rules of the game.

This belief also supports the New Age belief that God is the universe, making Him impersonal and more of a force or energy. When we know and believe that God is ever-present in our lives, our lives take on a new meaning. We understand that we are valuable and that there is a purpose for our existence. The chances that you were even born, according to several resources, are 1 in 400 trillion. Some scientists believe the odds of you being born were even 1 in 400 quadrillions. In short, the fact that you're even alive is nothing short of a miracle. This is why every life is precious, and we, as Christians, believe it has a purpose.

**Humanist Belief #2: Man is a part of nature and has emerged as a result of a continuous process.**

This belief supports the theory of evolution, which has never been proven on a macro level. Macroevolution has never been and can never be observed in our world because of the amount of time it would take to measure the entire process of one being becoming another. It is a law within nature that like produces like. If I plant a tomato seed, I certainly do not expect to reap an ear of corn. The same is true for living creatures in the air, land, and sea. You don't find one creature turning into a totally different creature. A dog does not become a cat, and a bird does not become a fish. Microevolution is true, and it is biblical. See the story of Noah and the flood as an example. Noah is commanded to take two of each kind or type of animal into the ark.[9] After the flood, it can be assumed that different variations of the same ancestor spread throughout the earth. Adaptation happens when you find that a living being has genetic changes in order to survive in the environment in which it lives. This is true, as you'll have dogs in Northern regions with much thicker fur than dogs who have adapted closer to the equator. This is what Darwin observed concerning the different variations of birds on the Galapagos Islands. Darwin's theory became obscured when his findings were applied at the macro level.

Darwinian evolution actually creates a sentiment of racism. I remember a girl in class recalling an encounter with an evolutionary exhibit at a museum that I will not name. She explains that the exhibits showed African Pygmies as being placed on the evolutionary chain as subhuman. She was extremely offended, and rightfully so. This would not be the only time that evolution was used to exterminate a people group. In fact, it was a core piece in the justification of European antisemitism in the early 1900s. Unfortunately, it goes to show that there is a racist sentiment established when looking at evolution in theory, and it is something I would highly encourage more research on the impact of this theory used to promote racism. This idea that gets to define what is and is not human. All of which directly oppose the Christian teaching that each individual life is valuable and unique. So much so that nobody else in the world has the same fingerprint as you.

The concept of a continuous process not only connects with the New Age religion, but it also fulfills a very important prophecy as laid out in the book of Daniel. The idea supports that man is in a constant state of evolution. With continued evolution eventually comes immortality through either breaking the karmic cycle of death and rebirth or through medical science. The book of Daniel saw a time when mankind would blend itself with machines. This doesn't feel too far off as most of our electronic devices are really extensions of ourselves, as Elon Musk describes. Daniel 2:43 speaks of a society where iron (machine) and clay (mankind) will try to mingle (come together), and this will be the state of the world prior to the return of Christ. Humanists play a big role in bringing that forward.

**Humanist Belief #3: Man's religious culture and civilization, as depicted by anthropology and history, are the product of a gradual development due to interaction with the natural environment and social heritage. The individual born into a particular culture is largely molded by that culture.**

This is true in some respects. We are influenced by how we are raised. I love the apple doesn't fall far from the tree euphemism. We say this when wanting to describe the reasoning behind why a person's behavior so closely reflects that of their parents. I like to respond with, "Of course, it doesn't; it was nourished by the tree." Christians go through a process of unlearning. We must unlearn the faulty rearing of our parents and learn, instead, the ways of God which lead us to greater peace, joy, and overall quality of life. Our upbringing does not dictate the course of our lives. We can powerfully put the past to rest and embrace a new life in Christ.

Matthew, for example, was no longer simply a tax collector. One interaction with Jesus and a command to follow was all it took to see a changed life.

However, there are some things that speak to humanity on a more universal level, regardless of what your cultural background believes them to be. All humans want to be loved; this is universal. All humans ask questions. There was a documentary I saw in high school which tracked the development of newborns through their first year of life. It didn't matter where they came from or what resources had; they all hit those developmental milestones and were walking by their first birthday. These are some commonalities that we can trace on a biological level.

From a social standpoint, we must look at some more commonalities. Regardless of upbringing, social status, culture, or religious belief, humans ask questions. Why was I born? Why do we die? Is there a God? We are able to hold intellectual conversations, and the complexity of spoken and written language is in itself a point of distinction between humans and animals. We have the ability to choose between right and wrong. This includes questioning what is and is not the right thing. These are some of the similarities we share as human beings. Although there are variations in belief based on history, the environment, and other factors, as the humanist belief suggests, there is an exception to the rule.

Some Christians follow Christ due to religious tradition. Humanity is inclined toward religiosity. A relationship with the risen Christ is very different. When you've encountered the supernatural love of God, your entire world changes. Paul, who was originally a Pharisee, took on a new identity and was no longer found killing Christians. I think he really serves as the best example to refute this point. The transformation from Saul to Paul was nothing short of miraculous. Saul was a result of his background. He was a top-notch zealot with hate in his heart for those who followed Jesus. He followed and taught every Jewish custom according to the law. A Pharisee to top all Pharisees. It took one encounter with the risen Christ for all of the memories, experiences, and cultural norms that once shaped him to become nothing in comparison to this newly revealed identity and truth. Paul explains this phenomenon in Philippians 3:5–8 (NKJV),

> Circumcised the eighth day, of the stock of Israel, of the tribe of Benjamin, a Hebrew of the Hebrews; concerning the law, a Pharisee; concerning zeal, persecuting the church; concerning the righteousness which is in the law, blameless. But what things were gain to me, these I have counted loss for Christ. Yet indeed I also count all things loss for the excellence of the knowledge of Christ Jesus my Lord, for whom I have suffered the loss of all things, and count them as rubbish, that I may gain Christ.

**Humanist Belief #4: The time has passed for theism, deism, modernism, and the several varieties of "new thought."**

This asserts that humanity no longer needs God. That we have come to a point where the belief in God is nothing more than a myth, and our intellectual evolution has eliminated the need for God. This is not a new thought; it is actually the exact lie that was told to us in the garden. It essentially asserts that we are gods and capable of running our own lives without God. It fuels our pride, which is the exact thing that gives birth to sin and separation from God. Theism, by definition, is the belief in a god or gods. This is an old way of thinking, according to the humanist. It places the modern human at the center of intellect and denies the existence of belief in a creator.

Deism, on the other hand, is the belief in the existence of a creator who does not intervene in the affairs of mankind. I believe deism was the first step toward atheism. This belief system was birthed out of the intellectual movements of the seventeenth and eighteenth centuries. This was the first step in bringing doubt to the minds of the people. When God becomes some impersonal force, people acknowledge His existence but have no desire to come to know Him. The God of the Bible is constantly revealing His character to and through humanity. You may be surprised to know that American forefathers like George Washington, John Adams, and Thomas Jefferson were deists. Some were even known as Christian deists. This is where history gets a bit confusing. Christians tend to get a bad reputation, and it is because of people who wear the title of Christian yet hold a belief in a god that is not involved with the affairs of humanity. They cannot be a Christian at all if they have not, on the most foundational level, been born again. An experience in which a human receives the gift of the Holy Spirit, enabling them to live out life according to the Christian values set before them. Other famous deists include Abraham Lincoln, Benjamin Franklin, Leonardo DaVinci, Thomas Edison, Thomas Pain, Voltaire, Mark Twain, and Johann Adam Weishaupt, just to name a few.

**Humanist Belief #5: Religious humanism considers the complete realization of human personality to be the end of man's life and seeks its development and fulfillment in the here and now. This is the explanation of the humanist's social passion.**

It is good to have a passion for social issues. A desire to want to do good things is evidence of a faith that is alive in Jesus Christ. However, this moves our focus from eternity to considering the consequences of right now. I believe being present at the moment is very important, but we need to understand that our decisions not only have temporary consequences but eternal ones as well. Atheism asserts that there is no eternity, and so the fullness of life's purpose is to develop yourself to be the best you can be. Our temporary pleasures, lifelong careers, and changing hobbies do not bring full development of our character. There are plenty of people who still feel immensely unfulfilled throughout their lives and even up until the end of their lives. For some, this means ending their life prematurely due to a lack of purpose.

I have felt this inner pull many times in my life that said I was meant to do something great. This is called being drawn into the fulfillment of your destiny. We are drawn in this way because we were created by God to fulfill a unique purpose on earth. A big part of the Christian life is seeking God for our divine purpose, which will lead to ultimate fulfillment in Christ. We would not fear or question death if this life and our achievements during our short lifetime were the ends of it all. There would be no question asking if the concept of eternity was not placed in our hearts. The Bible tells us to place our focus on eternity.[10]

**Humanist Belief #6: There will be no uniquely religious emotions and attitudes of the kind hitherto associated with belief in the supernatural.**

This is just a total denial of the existence of God. It denies the real-life changes that many born-again believers experience. This asserts that those experiences are not valid. People do see the supernatural invade the natural. There are myths, legends, ghost stories, and mysteries that talk about sublime experiences. The Christian would assert that these things were supernatural occurrences, most likely concerning angelic beings, including the demonic. God is very active; in fact, the Bible says that He never rests.[11] This means that the unseen is at work, influencing that which is seen. Unlike Hinduism, which speaks of an impersonal force or universal soul called the Brahman, the God of the Bible is extremely personal and not merely an unnamed force. We see miracles take place around the world and lives drastically changed by a God that intervenes in our affairs. The beautiful thing about Christianity is that you can take someone who committed heinous crimes and see the work of God soften and change their heart completely. Christians often carry a testimony. This is simply a witness as to what God has done in their lives. I would encourage you all to listen to people's testimonies as they will certainly encourage you and build your faith.

**Humanist Belief #7: Man will learn to face the crises of life in terms of his knowledge of their naturalness and probability. Reasonable and manly attitudes will be fostered by education**

**and supported by custom. We assume that humanism will take the path of social and mental hygiene and discourage sentimental and unreal hopes and wishful thinking.**

Have you ever had a bad day? What about a bad week? A bad month or year? Well, what if part of that bad time was coupled with a tragedy? One that you felt completely powerless to change. Most people in cases like this pray for a miracle. According to this belief, it is entirely up to you and your own limited knowledge to see yourself through hard times. To make matters worse, this belief supports the notion that we should not have high hopes, that we need to understand that tragedies happen and just be reasonable about it. There is nothing reasonable going through our minds when a crisis occurs. In fact, it is in times of suffering and when we are most weak that God shows Himself to be strong. It is in times like this that we must believe that a mustard seed can move a mountain. He is the God of the impossible. I love to hear stories of the cancer turnaround case or the miracle survival of a freak accident. It shows that miracles can and do happen. I also believe that there was a believing heart on the other side of that miracle, praying that God would, in fact, intervene. Had this person accepted the circumstances and moved on, we may not have seen that miracle.

So much of Christianity is built around having faith, which is the substance of things hoped for, the evidence of things not seen (Hebrews 1:11). There are countless lives that have been changed by this faith which goes completely against the rational mind at times. There is no logical way to explain some of these occurrences, and this proves that we cannot always trust solely on probability. Remember the statistic mentioned earlier about your birth. The probability that you would even be born is slim to none. Human life in itself is both a miracle and improbable. Miracles are improbable. God loves to show examples of improbability throughout the Bible. This takes the credit off of mankind and places it back on God. The Bible is full of examples where God used the people least qualified for a task to complete the assignment ahead. Moses, who had a stutter, was told to petition Pharaoh for the release of the Israelites. Paul used to murder Christians, then went on to be responsible for a good portion of the New Testament, church planting, and even being killed for the sake of the gospel. David was a young shepherd boy, yet he slew Goliath, the giant, with only a rock and a sling. He later became king of Israel, although the people had initially favored Saul and discounted David. Sarah was barren yet bore Isaac in her old age. She laughed at the thought of having a child, and God asked why she laughed because nothing was impossible for Him. Joseph was sold into slavery by his brothers, falsely accused by his master's wife, and forgotten by the prisoners. Yet God used all of this as a preparation to give him the highest title. He would sit and reign in the Pharaoh's position.

All of this is to say that it doesn't matter how much education, reason, statistical data, or outside knowledge we have. God can fill in our weakness with His strength and use us to do amazing things.[12] It seems very cynical to live a life that says we should have no hope or wishful thinking. What is a life that cannot hope in the face of tragedy? We should think big, dream big, and hope big because we serve a big God that can do big things.

**Humanist Belief #8: The goal of humanism is a free and universal society in which people voluntarily and intelligently cooperate for the common good. Humanists demand a shared life in a shared world.**

To understand the fullness of this belief, one could write an entire book. At one point in America, certain beliefs and groups were considered to be detestable because of the things they were doing. This would include harming children and animals and performing cruel ritualistic acts in order to practice their beliefs openly. In the world of the humanist, each person sets their own compass for morality, and so the demand of a shared life in a shared world removes certain restrictions. You will notice issues such as sexualizing minors and, in some cases, children as young as four years old becoming increasingly normal. As media expands, the age limit seems to decrease in terms of tolerance and exposure. The separation of church and state was initially in place to protect religious liberty. This was considered a win for Christians, but it can be equally applied to groups who are against what Christianity represents. That being said, all things that look great on the surface may not always be so. For the humanist, it is more fitting for groups who are pictured as developing the self and not engaging in the affairs of others. This follows the logic of English occultist Aleister Crowley's *Law of Thelema*. In other words, this law claims that we are to "do what thou wilt and that shall be the whole of the law," whereas the Christian believes that love is the fulfillment of the law. One is purposely self-focused, while the other focuses on the needs of others.

Christianity, at its core, prioritizes bringing others into the kingdom of God through spreading the message of the gospel. It is largely concerned with doing and standing for what is right according to the inner conviction of the Holy Spirit. It is very difficult to know what is the common good for the humanist. During a time of war, the common good may have been to fight the war at the expense of the rights of some individuals. However, now we see more examples of groups who have been marginalized as the center of education reform. The humanist sees this as an opportunity for inclusivity while perpetuating the victim and villain narrative. According to a very linear historical timeline, the stories told around these groups are very one-sided to represent a type of victimhood. It is this state of victimhood in which many of these groups are represented, therefore, placing them at a further disadvantage. Rather than recognizing their value for positive contribution to society, always looming over them is the oppression, pain, loss, suffering, and anguish of their past. Now that we have explored some of the main points of the Humanist Manifesto, we can discuss how these thoughts have permeated education.

# Roots Run Deep

But of the tree of the knowledge of good and evil you shall not eat, for in the day that you eat of it you shall surely die.

Genesis 2:17 (NKJV)

At first glance, the ideological concept of humanism seems benevolent. How can something centered around humans not be good? It would seem logical that this is the very thing that society needs to self-correct. Humanism is the open door to agnosticism and, in many cases, atheism. The grasp of humanism is strong in our schools. The ideology permeates nearly every aspect of education, and I believe this is one of the biggest factors in the annihilation of faith. Despite what some may try to tell you, humanism is a religion birthed out of the Renaissance (rebirth) period. Although it claims to be anti-religion and secular in nature, it is a religion. By definition, religion is a particular system of faith and worship. Faith is simply belief and trust. When we trust something enough to guide our lives, we are placing our faith in it. Christianity calls for faith in Jesus Christ to govern and guide our lives. Humanism calls for faith in the self, medical science, and technology to solve all the world's problems. It seems quite illogical to put your faith into humanity to solve the very problems that it has created. You may have heard the euphemism, "I am losing faith in humanity." Well, you would have to put faith into humanity in order for it to be lost. It is an attractive belief system because it speaks to our Adamic (fleshly) nature through which we seek to govern ourselves. It is the same rebellious nature that comes into agreement with humanist thought. This is how the same household names in science, philosophy, literature, and other subjects maintain influence over the populace. Atheistic humanism denies the need for God, and we can trace its roots back to the earliest days of human history when man fought to be the center of all things—where humanity sought to become a god. Let's explore a list of those household names. Some of the names may shock you, and we can be sure that this list is not exhaustive.

### Literature

Some of the most influential humanists in literature include big names like Margaret Atwood. Atwood is well known for her novel *The Handmaid's Tale*. A story that promotes reproductive rights and deals directly with the abortion debate. She paints society under Christian theocracy as a dictatorship that oppresses the rights of women. My co-teacher insisted on reading this with our eleventh-grade class during my first year of teaching. My stomach was in knots as she described what was truly a dystopia and misrepresentation of the Christian faith. Another prominent figure was Betty Friedan. She wrote *The Feminine Mystique*, which sparked the second wave of feminism in America. Daniel Handler, also known as Lemony Snicket, wrote a popular children's series called *A Series of Unfortunate Events*, which exposes children to several dark themes and explores betrayal, instability, and death. Popular titles include *The Hostile Hospital*, *The Carnivorous Carnival*, and *The Reptile Room*. Zora Neale Hurston is another popular humanist who wrote about the issue of race and gender, with one of her more popular books being titled *Their Eyes Were Watching God*. The popular novel and movie series *Harry Potter* was written by the infamous humanist, J. K. Rowling. The series really serves as an entry point into witchcraft, yet, it is a beloved story across multiple generations. Other well-known humanist authors include Aldous Huxley, Niccolo Machiavelli, Ayn Rand, Alice Walker, Mark Twain, Walt Whitman, Kurt Vonnegut, and more.

**Science**

Unfortunately, the idea of creationism is not even really up for debate in most areas of academia. This is thanks to household names in science like Richard Dawkins. He is one of the most well-known self-proclaimed agnostics and a favorite go-to resource for modern atheists. Another well-known humanist is the late Stephen Hawking. He denied the existence of God and is a celebrated name in theoretical physics and cosmology. Modern practices in the psychiatric field can thank the infamous humanist, Sigmund Freud. Freud believed that belief in God was the unconscious mind's need for wish fulfillment, that humans needed to feel secure, and so they choose to believe in God as a powerful father figure. Many of you may be familiar with Bill Nye, the science guy. Bill Nye was a huge influence on millennials and is a strong believer in evolution. Other scientists to note include Albert Einstein, Jerome Isaac Friedman, Carl Sagan, and Neil deGrasse Tyson.

## Philosophy

Perhaps one of the most mind-boggling classes is philosophy. Some of the teachings are really difficult to wrap your mind around because you need to be able to follow the philosopher's line of thinking. This is the class that probably bred the most doubt in my mind. Friedrich Nietzsche is well known for his book *God is Dead*. He believed that the Enlightenment period eliminated the need for God. The Age of Enlightenment was an intellectual movement that placed focus on scientific discoveries, inventions, new laws, and political revolutions. The true history and founding principles of the United States are more closely aligned to Enlightenment thinking than Christian ideology which is a commonly retold lie in history classes. Enlightenment is more of a celebration of the freeing of the mind from the shackles of religion. It is the fullness of the serpents lie in the Garden of Eden and the basis of belief for secret societies. If you would only eat of this forbidden knowledge, you would be like God. You will be enlightened. Other notable humanist philosophers include Auguste Comte, John Dewey, Bertrand Russell, and Jean-Paul Sartre.

## History

I've heard it said before that history is really his-story. The funny thing about teaching history is that the textbooks do a great job of placing a certain spin on the pieces that are included in our education. The companies who compile the textbooks use a fine-tooth comb to ensure that some pieces are left out. Unfortunately, you need all of the parts to tell a full story, and anything that goes against the approved narrative doesn't make the cut. I remember specifically teaching the Reconstruction period to eighth-grade students in New York City. The textbook flamed the race issue but failed to mention the true economic destruction of the South. This painted a very one-sided picture of history. One that would lead students to compartmentalize people's motives during this time period. The people in the North were good and opposed slavery, while the folks in the South were evil racists. This narrative still plays out today, but it denies the truth of the complexity of the time period. This is only one of many examples.

Some well-known historical figures were Friedrich Engles and Karl Marx. They co-authored *The Communist Manifesto*. When communism is actually applied in nations such as China and the USSR, we see a loss of human rights, total governmental control, and an extreme loss of life. When it comes to the education system, communism is not packaged this way. It hits a very real nerve in the hearts of the people who see the impact of crony capitalism. I am not talking about real capitalism, where you have healthy market competition, but more or less what is practiced today. You have big corporate conglomerates that, in many ways, take advantage of the working class and, in some cases, use foreign slave labor. Furthermore, Marx believed that religion is a creation of society and Marxist Leninist atheism proposes that religion is like opium to the people. Opium is a very powerful drug. In theory, Marxism denies God. Other important historical humanists were Nikola Tesla, Abraham Maslow, and Madalyn Murray O'Hair. O'Hair was single-handedly one of the most influential women responsible for removing God from schools. A society is set for destruction when it removes God from the equation, and each person becomes the pilot of their own destiny according to their own moral compass. This seems liberating, but when you understand the human condition from a Christian perspective, the idea is actually quite frightening.

### Media and Other Topics

Media is one of the most influential tools for either good or manipulation. Hollywood and mainstream news outlets choose which social and political issues will be the focus of the day. The likability of celebrities also tells the mind that you can trust them. We trust what we find attractive. In recent years, the media has done such a great job at creating a deeper societal divide. Once you've chosen sides, it doesn't really matter what they say because it's likely that you'll believe it regardless. Well-known actors like Steve Allen, Kristen Bell, Jodie Foster, Paul Giamatti, Kathy Griffin, Penn Jillette, Kiera Knightley, Hugh Laurie, Seth MacFarlane, Julianne Moore, Ellen Page, Daniel Radcliffe, and Charlie Chaplin. There are a lot more names that can be included here, but honestly, it doesn't take much to look at some of the movies coming out of Hollywood to see where they stand. On the political front, you have secular humanist Bill Maher, who constantly has Christians as the target of his jokes. Another lesser-known humanist is Ann Dunham. You may have never heard of her. However, you might know her son, Barak Obama. These are just a few examples; there are many more that can be researched.

## Overall Impact

A quick internet search when studying a new philosopher, scientist, author, media influencer, or other personality in history will reveal a lot about their views and how their work has been impacted. This is a good practice that would be wise to adopt. We should seek to know more about the person we are learning about. I've always felt that a quick read of the person's biography would reveal quite a bit about their work. Their beliefs are sure to influence the work that they produce. Equipping yourself with this added information helps during group discussions when making a claim concerning why you may not agree with their work. Please let that sink in. You do not have to agree, and that doesn't make you ignorant or hateful. There is this odd unspoken idea that when sitting under the teaching of a professor, we must take all things said as fact. That's at least what I used to feel. This cannot be further from the truth.

I advise you to take note of something known as the Chameleon Effect. This describes a phenomenon where we begin to mimic those around us. This is also true for the stories we read and the media we consume. It's the reason why after watching a spy movie, you suddenly wanted to become one. Hollywood does a great job at glamorizing the humanist agenda because writers and producers understand the power of monkey see monkey do. It explains why social media influencers are able to get such a high number of followers. They have a core set of people who want to copy what they do, speak how they speak, and wear what they wear. How much more can we see this impact on the development of the human brain and, ultimately, the factors that motivate society?

Understanding the deeply held beliefs of the people we learn about removes the confusion behind the many voices. It gives us the ability to decide whether or not we agree with their viewpoints. We can understand more clearly that the scientific conclusions drawn, the inspiration behind the literature, the movies that are made, and even the way that history is told can be manipulated to support a certain way of thinking. What is even more astonishing is that this way of thinking claims itself to be secular and without belief. Collectively, it misrepresents God and, in some cases, denies His existence altogether. In this next section, we will explore the beliefs of the humanist to better understand how it has shaped their worldview to be in direct opposition to the truth concerning the God of the Bible. You may also find that your beliefs align with humanistic thought. In fact, I would be surprised to know that you didn't share at least one belief because it has been so deeply ingrained into our education.

# Digging Deeper

Not everyone who says to Me, "Lord, Lord," shall enter the kingdom of heaven, but he who does the will of My Father in heaven.

Matthew 7:21 (NKJV)

Let's dig a little bit deeper into the courses of study nearly every student must go through. Have you ever wondered who picks the subjects and why? There is a level of interconnectivity in the subjects. The little country schoolhouse used to teach reading, writing, and arithmetic. At one point, there were several vocational schools that taught students real-life skills that they could transfer into a career or apply to their lives. Gone are the days of home economics and shop classes. A big part of the modern selection of study includes history, philosophy, fine arts, and English, as courses referred to as encompassing the humanities. These subjects can show the fullness of human expression, and we can learn a lot about humanity. What I found to be most confusing was studying these subjects without a fuller picture of the world around me. I didn't have the full story. There were hidden histories and spiritual truths of which I was not yet made aware. New Age beliefs refer to the awakening to these truths as the woke movement. Being woke is not the same as having the truth in Christ revealed to you.

**Are They Really Christians?**

The Bible tells us that the wisdom of the world is foolishness to God. Our wisdom must come from God because He is infinite in thought, and we are finite.[13] When Solomon sought God's wisdom, God rewarded him, and he was known as a very wise king. The book of Proverbs has much of Solomon's wisdom recorded. The humanities involve learning about different philosophical approaches, especially those of the Greeks. However, the Bible warns us about this type of thinking which conforms your mind to the thinking pattern of the world and not as God thinks.[14] Certain types of philosophical thought welcome in doubt. The enemy of faith is unbelief. Lies are the seeds planted into our minds, watered by doubt which ultimately grows unbelief. One of the first real shifts I felt in my thinking was when I watched a movie called *Agora* in class. The movie highlighted the tensions between the Greeks and the early Christians. This was yet again another gross misrepresentation of the interactions between the two groups. Christians were made out to be these crazy people burning things down and beating Greeks for their wisdom. You can read about the ways in which Paul traveled to Greece preaching the gospel in peace, such as in Acts 17. Jesus told His disciples on many occasions to remain in peace, and Paul tells us to make peace with all. The movie was meant to highlight that Christians should be stopped and that they were the aggressors toward the peaceful Greeks. For any Christian group that thinks raping, beating, and killing is the proper response for evangelism, then the Bible would claim that you do not know God because He is the expression of love. There are many other examples in history of unregenerate men and women using the name of Christianity to further human means. These are referred to as false converts in the Bible, and they are frequently addressed. There will be some who claim Christianity, yet Christ says they will be turned away from Him on the day of judgment, stating that He never knew them.[15] Not everyone who says they are Christian is a good representation of the faith, nor are they all actually in the faith. That is not necessarily a good reason to turn your back on following Jesus. The point I am trying to make is that when you read about different people, groups, and theories, do a little research. If the person holds atheistic beliefs, you can bet that the work they produce will follow suit. When you read about dictators in history, do a little research. I can assure you that the morals that motivated the person played a big role in the atrocities that followed. I say this because there are gaps in our education. Not everything is covered in the classroom, and sometimes those missing puzzle pieces can make all the difference in our understanding.

## Historical Perspective

It is easy to say that religion is the biggest problem in the world, and without it, we would all be better off. I would agree to an extent. Religion was created by man, so naturally, we know it will, in fact, fail as other human attempts to solve the world's problems have failed. This faith is not a religion; it is a working relationship with Jesus Christ. I can understand, though, why some would feel no need to look any further into Christianity, judging from a religious point of view. One look at the Crusades, and any non-believer has heard enough about what they believe to be the Christian faith. The problem is that Jesus Christ would have been against everything concerning the actions of the crusaders. The other problem is that if you don't know Jesus Christ, you will associate the two as being synonymous. Just because evil men do things in the name of someone else doesn't mean the two should ever have been associated, nor does it reflect the teachings present within the faith. The Crusades involved raping, pillaging, and killing, all in the name of Christianity. Nowhere in the Bible does it say to take up your sword and act like crazed animals for the forgiveness of sins and eternal glory despite what Pope Urban II told them. It does say to love your enemies and pray for those who persecute you.[16] When Peter took up his sword and cut off the ear of the high priest in the Garden of Gethsemane, Jesus stopped him and said if you live by the sword, you'll die by the sword.[17] Your history teacher doesn't tell you that part of the story, though. The history teacher fails to mention the political gains to be had and the use of false promises to gain influence and expand. Nobody corrects the actions of the crusaders and says that the Bible doesn't teach that, nor would it ever say that what they did was right or even remotely biblical.

Let me take a moment and say the words for you. What about the Old Testament? There was a lot of killing happening there, right? Yes, that's right. There is also a lot of missing context. A more in-depth study would reveal the heinous treatment of Israelites during this time period. The vile practices performed by neighboring civilizations included everything from sacrificing human babies, burning people alive, and sodomizing children. If we really want to talk about torture, the Romans were well known for various means of capital punishment, like crucifixion. There are other examples in the Bible of ruthless leaders like Pharaoh in Egypt and King Herod, who called for the slaughtering of infants. People will point to Psalm 137:9 (ESV), which says, "Blessed shall he be who takes your little ones and dashes them against the rock!" They use this to say, "Look, that God is crazy and bloodthirsty." The truth is that the psalmist was using this visual as an example of praying that God would render to their enemies what had been done to them. That is part of human expression, to want justice for the atrocities that have been committed. When we read about bloodshed in the Bible, we need a fuller historical picture to understand what was actually happening and who were the true aggressors.

There were many civilizations that have been at war with biblical Israel historically. The Assyrians were particularly ruthless and frequently waged wars against surrounding nations. They were well known for this behavior and feared for their military power. They don't teach you this when studying ancient civilizations. We do, however, learn about their gods, goddesses, holy days, and achievements. Wars are a part of life on Earth until the fullness of the redemption of all things. God promises to fight our battles. I love the layered meaning behind the Bible. Although there are literal examples, there is so much that is also allegorical. The physical enemies that Israel fought represented the very real spiritual enemies that we face. The very real battles to receive the land promised to

God's children. A place of peace and rest in the soul and land when we enter into eternity. Where we receive all of the blessings prepared for us from the foundation of the earth. It is a return to Eden.

When we learn about God's true character, we don't see a ruthless dictator who was moody and wanted to slaughter humanity. We instead see a loving, protective Father who would go to great lengths to protect His children. This was true for Old Testament Israel and for New Testament believers. Just like ancient Israel was persecuted in many respects, the early Christians were also persecuted.

Most of your history classes will not cover the persecution of Christians. Historically, the Roman Empire was well known for persecuting Christians. Some noteworthy examples include the reign of Nero and his persecution of Christians in 64 AD and the reign of Diocletian and the Great Christian Persecution, which took place from 303 AD to 311 AD. These are not the only examples, as Paul recounts spending many nights in Roman prisons. This went on until a political move by Emperor Constantine in 313 AD made Christianity the official religion of Rome. We credit this with being when the true movement of Christians was now more largely accepted and spread throughout the earth, but not by means of true faith, but rather by means of imperialistic rage. When the Edict of Milan was issued, pure Christian doctrine was blended with Roman Pagan worship. This continued for hundreds of years and led to several wars between the Roman Catholic church and the early Protestants in England and surrounding territories during what is known as the Protestant Reformation.

Well, I wasn't born an Israelite, and I'm not chosen. The enemy loved using that one against me to create a picture of God that does not line up with who He is. God chose a people group to represent Him on the earth. This was done so that the acts of His power could be recorded in history, and the lineage pointing to Jesus would show the fulfillment of hundreds, even thousands of years of prophecies. This was the factor that would separate God from all of the other gods created by humans in the image of humans. It is through Jesus that we are born again in Spirit and brought into the lineage of chosen Israel. Their history becomes our history, and a clear picture of God's love for the whole world becomes clearer. We see more precisely stories of women like Ruth, Tamar, Rahab, and Bathsheba who were not of Israel lineage yet were brought in and are included in the genealogy leading to the birth of the Messiah.

History is often told from the viewpoint of the victors. The minority voice is silenced. I've heard it once said that history is his-story. Get it? It is often biased and told from a singular point of view. The book of Daniel gives us a clearer insight into the history of the world through the interpretation of a dream by King Nebuchadnezzar. It shows us five different kingdoms.[18] Each of these kingdoms with a history of slavery, persecution, class conflict, and dictatorship. The Bible refers to them as Gentile kingdoms in the world. Simply meaning, not governed by God. The Israelites, though biblically speaking a physical people, represent God's chosen people, those governed by God. Through Jesus Christ, this includes you and me regardless of physical lineage. This is why Scripture says we are in the world, but we are not of the world. We don't conform to the pattern of the world, as we see that time and time again, history is bound to repeat itself. Why? The human capacity to solve the world's problems is limited because we as humans are limited. The end result is always war, famine, disease, persecution, pestilence, and so on. This goes back to identifying the issue as being a problem within the heart of mankind. A problem that only God can change. Daniel goes on to describe this final kingdom, of the crushing rock kingdom of Christ, where there will be no more tears, pain, or death.[19]

I have heard it said before that Christians were never persecuted. Though this is not true, it reflects the truth of a gap present within our history classes. One might consider the fate of the early apostles. They were either beheaded, crucified, hung, stoned, or placed in boiling oil. The purpose of this book is not a history lesson but to equip you with truths when confronted with discussions concerning these topics. There are Christians today who congregate in underground churches in places like China and some Middle Eastern countries where radical Islam is intolerant toward religious freedoms. This area of study is pertinent as Christianity has been in many respects deemed hateful and intolerant. The truth is that the world has been, in fact, hateful and intolerant toward Christianity.

## Literary Perspective

Mythology is highly fascinating for many. Various mythologies from around the world are studied as classrooms explore the backstories of the gods and goddesses of the ancient world. From a Christian worldview, the gods of the ancient world share a connection with fallen angels. Some believe that the worship of these gods actually represents the worship of fallen angels revealing themselves to mankind as gods. Some Christian circles believe that the gods you read about today are essentially repurposed from the same pantheon of gods, only changing to fit the cultural needs of the region. A popular duo referenced in the Bible is Baal and Asherah. Celebrities have been seen wearing costumes that reflect the ancient male or female deity or showing their symbols in music videos, movies, TV shows, interviews, and other mediums of expression. The Baal and Asherah are also represented as the gods of the sun and the moon. This example reflects a representation of the Canaanite gods. Another example is the Babylonian myth of the goddess Ishtar; having been impregnated by the rays of the sun from the sun god, she gave birth to Tammuz, the morning star, during the winter solstice. These stories from mythology have made their way into mainstream Christianity and are often mistaken as the pure representation of the faith. The Bible even makes mentions giants as being the hybrid offspring of fallen angels and human beings. These mixed beings were worshipped in pagan cultures as feasts were made for them, children were sacrificed to them, and the people built temples in which to worship them. Today references to fallen angels and their hybrid offspring have crept into popular culture as aliens and ascended masters. Whether they are called the ancient Anunnaki or the Greek gods of Olympus, the reference to these creatures remains the same in literary tradition. For the Greeks, the gods are personified in Ovid's

71

*Metamorphoses*; for the Babylonians, it's *The Epic of Gilgamesh*; for the Egyptians, it's the many hieroglyphs recorded on papyrus. Regardless of cultural background, the honored forces remain the same but change identity to fit the needs of the people. Further examples of this difference include that of the goddess of motherhood and fertility. Today you might see her honored on the cup of a well-loved coffee company. The Lady of the Sea printed in green on the white cup. This was Asherah in some Middle Eastern traditions. For the Egyptians, this was Isis. The Celts called her Brigid. Hindus call her Shakti. Norse mythologies record her as Freya. The Chinese have named her Mazu. The Sumerians refer to her as Inanna. Finally, she is more modernly known by her Greco-Roman identity as Aphrodite or Venus. This is one example of how the same goddess made her way through cultures but what she represents remains fairly consistent. The mythology around these gods of the ancient world is front and center in literary study and taught as early as kindergarten.

Some use these examples to say that these religions have been around far longer than Christianity. Though this is true, the stories compiled are really nothing more than a knock-off to the true plan of redemption. They are kind of like the guy selling purses on the corner in Manhattan. It looks like the real thing until you realize it's missing a piece of the logo or the sewing isn't done well. The Bible teaches that the plan of salvation had been written before the foundation of the earth. This is a hard one for some to understand. In fact, some believe that the fallen angel rebellion happened prior to the creation of man and that mankind would be the vehicle through which God would save the world. There are a lot of theories, but that is just one.

The Bible is, in fact, one of the most consistent representations of the initial coming of the Messiah as well as telling of His return. Those who lack understanding in this area will claim that the Bible contradicts. When you understand Jesus, you can read the Bible, especially the old prophecies which were hundreds and, in some cases, thousands of years apart, and see the pattern of consistency. You will also see that the New Testament reflects a fulfillment of the Old Testament prophecies. The revelation of the knowledge of Jesus Christ shows all of the Old Testament stories to be an archetype for Jesus as Messiah, Son of God, Teacher, Counselor, Healer, Judge, Redeemer, our Sacrifice, and so much more!

God has a funny way of creatively placing His hand on everything you can possibly imagine. YHWH is the revealed name of God. In Hebrew, the writing is read backward from that of Western writing. In Hebrew, it would look more like HWHY. When you transfer the name of God, also referred to as the Tetragrammaton in its most ancient of languages, Paleo Hebrew, the representation of the symbols is actually read Hand Behold Nail Behold. Only to be fulfilled by Jesus in His crucifixion on the cross. The name of God was revealed in biblical history well before Jesus' birth. There are so many examples like this, including the actual written prophecies which point to Jesus as the Messiah. You come to realize that He really is the Word made manifest.

**Early Texts**

My scope of study while in college included English literature, sociology, and history. My thesis was based on finding common threads in mythologies around the world spread apart by different time periods. I worked my way through several sources, including *Gilgamesh*, *Beowulf*, the *Iliad*, the *Odyssey*, the *Aeneid*, *Dante's Divine Comedy*, and so much more. I wanted to know the truth. The missing puzzle piece for me was the Bible. I wanted to know why *Beowulf* and *Gilgamesh* both mentioned the flood. A story that the Bible also mentioned. How is it possible to account for these events across different periods of time where some civilizations would have very little interaction? I also asked myself, why was the story worth recording and sharing what had been recorded? I then began to question the validity of the Bible. How is it possible that a Norse epic and a Sumero-Akkadian epic could have such similarities? It is not likely that these groups mingled as *Beowulf* and *Gilgamesh* are amongst the oldest written accounts and far removed both geographically and linguistically. I then came to realize that other civilizations shared the flood account, including that of some Native American tribes. I became familiar with the Judeo-Christian account in childhood and never wrote it off as simply mythology. There was something fascinating about it, and upon further research, I came to find that this event really did change the trajectory of the world. It only further piqued my interest in the biblical account, which seemed to be the most detailed and comprehensive. So much of the world today tries to play the Bible off as a work of fiction when, in fact, it holds historical, allegorical, metaphorical, and literal life-changing truths. It's a literary masterpiece, to say the least.

Apart from a literary lens, the Bible has power. There is power to transform and change lives with lasting change. The truth of the condition of mankind is represented throughout that book. The truth of history is in that book. The truth of every philosophical question is in that book. How can this be so? It is the living Word of God. When you receive God's Spirit, the Bible comes alive. You begin to feel as though God is speaking directly into your soul through the words on the page. This occurrence is God guiding you to exactly what you need in exactly the right moment. God speaks directly to us through His Word.[20] It is the Word of God that must be revealed to us. People often struggle to understand the Bible because many of its truths must be revealed to us through the knowledge of Jesus Christ in a working relationship.

Paul is a great example of the power of the revelation of the Word of God. Everything that he thought he knew about being a Hebrew scholar was worth nothing in comparison to what he came to know as the truth through Christ. I was a good student. I graduated from college in the top 1 percent of my class. The crazy thing is that when I came to the Word of God, I realized that I knew nothing. I felt like Paul. When I say everything I was taught became useless in my mind compared to the life-changing truths revealed in God's Word, I mean everything.[21] God's strength is made perfect through our weaknesses. He is able to get the most glory when the situation is impossible for the person. If it were possible to do something in our own strength, then God would not get the glory because we would naturally take credit. This applies to our knowledge of understanding the Bible.

Most people cannot understand the Word of God. This is because the truth needs to be revealed to them. Many intellectuals like to claim that the Bible is full of contradictions, when in fact, this reveals the genius and divine inspiration of the text. It does not contradict whatsoever. Though it does have many different authors, its consistency relies on the fact that the writers were all led by the same Spirit. It is the Holy Spirit that comes and reveals these hidden truths. It remains consistent from Genesis to Revelation. Although the writers would have been removed from each other by both time and region, the consistency of the story of redemption would be interwoven through every fiber of the Word of God. What you come to learn is that everything points to Jesus Christ. The prophecies remain consistent in every last detail, and if we use probability, we can say that human error would be likely. People often point to the variety of translations as a source of error. What most fail to realize is that the English language evolved rapidly over the course of a thousand years. The English of the 1066 Norman Invasion is far different from the 1611 King James English. Even more so, there are not always accurate translations that enrapture the fullness of the meaning behind the Hebrew or Koine Greek in which the Bible was translated. This, however, does not imply that the overall message errs. In fact, the consistency of the message of Jesus Christ as a compilation of several authors removed by time and space would speak to its validity rather than it being the sole work of human beings. It truly is the divinely inspired Word of God.

## Philosophical Perspective

There is a particular school of thought that has most confused and complicated our society. The school of thought is called post-modernism. Pre-modernism allowed for the idea that God was responsible for creation and played a role in our lives to be viable. Modernism saw society as constantly progressing and man consistently evolving. Post-modernism takes away the notion of absolute truth. There is no absolute truth, and each individual's reality is only their version of the truth. This school of thought is most loved by atheists and secular humanists, which contrasts directly with the Christian notion that there is one truth, and it is Jesus Christ. This way of thinking opened the door to the acceptance of situational ethics in our society. You will see situational ethics practiced in our schools, on our news headlines, in politics, in courts, and in our personal lives. Many people see hot-button issues such as abortion as acceptable depending on the context surrounding the situation. A real example is that in the case of communism. It was acceptable to kill millions of innocent people for the greater good of enforcing a new economic system. This philosophical thought made room for the end justifying the means. The question we must ask is who is making the rules behind what is good and what is not? Who gets to define the greater good? These questions matter because, in order to create the world of "tolerance" and "inclusivity" that secular humanists want, the "old" ways of thinking have to be destroyed, and this includes anybody who refuses to part from their belief in Christian values.

Situational ethics is everywhere, and you might be surprised to have found yourself practicing this way of thinking. A popular news story was the case of Gypsy Rose Blanchard in 2015. She was the girl that everyone believed to be physically sick, and her mother was very controlling over her life, forcing her to pretend to have various illnesses. Gypsy and her boyfriend participated in the murder of her mother. Some say that she was justified in doing this because of the years of abuse that she had endured. This is a form of situational ethics. Gypsy is serving time in prison and has admitted that her mother did not deserve to be murdered. Repaying evil for evil never brings peace, happiness, change, or justice. In fact, it shows the dire need for mental and emotional healing. True healing can only begin when we engage in forgiveness.[22] In fact, some medical professionals have included forgiveness as part of their cancer patients' treatments to aid in the process of healing. When we forgive, we release both ourselves and those who have hurt us from bondage. The idea that it is justified to repay evil for evil on a situational basis is supported by the humanist philosophy of situation ethics.

The Bible teaches moral absolutes. This means that something is always either morally correct or incorrect. The Bible sets a standard far above what we as humans believe to be correct. The standard is perfection because God is perfect. However, we are not expected to reach this standard by human means. It is impossible to do so. God has always been concerned with the attitude of the heart. He is not impressed with appearances of right behavior because He judges that which is inside, not what is on the outside. To understand God's standard for morality, we were given the ten commandments by Moses. Violation of these laws is, ultimately, what hurts our world, and it is in our human nature to do them. Remember, the world looks the way it does as a result of sin entering into our world. The ten commandments were given so that we could see where we fall short of living in the right relationship with God and mankind. We can live in the right relationships when we are rooted in love. Love fulfills the law. So I ask again, was Gypsy justified? If we consider this justice, then what we are saying is that, sometimes, it is okay to murder. Murder should never be acceptable because we are not the ones who gave that life. We act in the role of God when we decide to end the life of another. That is for God to decide, not us. The Bible calls us to turn the other cheek and to grow in grace. It is always helpful to put yourself in the other person's shoes because then we consider how we would want to be treated.[23] In doing so, God grows compassion into our hearts for others rather than a need to obtain justice.

The Graham Staines story is an amazing example of forgiveness and surrendering justice into God's hands. Staines, his wife, and his children had been living in India as Christian missionaries. They cared for Indians in the region who were dealing with a disease called leprosy. Due to high racial and religious tensions in the region, a Hindu fundamentalist group became responsible for burning Staines and his two young sons, aged ten and six, to death. Gladys Staines had a choice. She chose to forgive. According to situation ethics, she had every right to hurt the tribal group responsible for the death of her husband and sons. That would never have truly settled the score.

Instead, she is quoted in an affidavit saying, "[...] It is far from my mind to punish the persons who were responsible for the death of my husband Graham and my two children. But it is my desire and hope that they would repent and be reformed." Gladys understood that a mind unredeemed is apt to bring pain and suffering. She understood that this person so badly needed to encounter the love of Christ. She understood that this was not her battle and that God was with her. She understood that Graham and her children were with God and that repaying these people for what they had done would not bring her family back together. She understood that by forgiving them, she would commit justice into the hands of God and remain in peace. Can you say you would have done the same?

Another incredible example of where situation ethics could apply but was not seen through was the case of Elisabeth Elliot. Her husband had gone on a missionary trip to Ecuador in 1956. He was killed by members of the Waorani tribe, making her a widow and her daughter now fatherless. Elliot could have become bitter and demanded that justice be served. She had every right according to situational ethics. Instead, she went right back to that tribe just two years later with her three-year-old daughter. She stayed with the tribe and sought to understand why they killed her husband. She continued the work that her husband had set out to do. She chose to try to understand them, and this produced compassion within her. Ms. Elliot wrote in *Life* magazine in 1961, "The Auca was trying to preserve his own way of life, his own liberty. He believed the foreigners were a threat to that liberty, so he feels he had every right to kill them. In America, we decorate a man for defending his country." Those are some pretty powerful words. Despite what she could have done or how she could have felt, she chose to forgive and seek to understand. That has made a world of a difference.

# Diversity and Inclusion

Every way of a man is right in his own eyes, But the Lord
weighs the hearts.

Proverbs 21:2 (NKJV)

There is a big push in the education system for diversity and
inclusion. There is even a course that you have to take when going
through teacher training that centers on this topic. For some of you
reading, a diverse population might be common. Other readers
may have experienced a culture shock if they come from a region
that is mostly homogenous to one or two cultural groups. Diversity
includes a range of identifying factors, and culture is only one piece.
You will encounter different religions, lifestyles, ways of thinking,
and experiences. Many of these social markers will be connected to
identity. We will unpack identity in a later chapter. In my opinion,
diversity is a great thing. I believe the kingdom of heaven is diverse.
Revelation 7:9 (NKJV) gives us a decent picture of heavenly diversity,

> After these things I looked, and behold, a great multitude
> which no one could number, of all nations, tribes, peoples,
> and tongues, standing before the throne and before the
> Lamb, clothed with white robes.

We see that God is quite creative because our differences are what
make us unique. We are all uniquely different, yet the body of Christ
is unified as one church in the Spirit. We are all uniquely created yet

equally loved by God. We all have a unique story yet remain united in our testimony to the power of God. Diversity is a great thing.

**Religious Diversity**

Unfortunately, the way that diversity is celebrated in school is typically in support of the coexist narrative. It is a narrative that teaches that we must exist together through tolerance regardless of belief. Not only is it illogical, as certain religions call for the annihilation of others, but it is irrational. I want to use Islam as an example. I would like to preface this by saying, I have had conversations with Muslims I respect. I have also read a fair portion of the Quran for myself, so I am not speaking from a position of ignorance. When we have competing ideologies, it is not possible to simply coexist. There will be a voice silenced in exchange for a voice heard. For example, Islam has been celebrated in recent years due to its prior experience with Islamophobia post 9/11. The Quran refers to all non-converts as infidels and proposes that conversion must take place at all costs. While Christianity does proselytize, it does not call for violence or force to accomplish its goals. We have previously covered the actions of those who called for violence in the name of Christianity, yet the main issue was that they were going against the teachings of Jesus. You would not take an example such as the American terrorist group Ku Klux Klan as a proper representation of Christianity. In the same regard, I would not say that ISIS is a proper representation of Islam. The difference between the KKK and ISIS is that ISIS is actually following the extremist commands outlined in the Quran, while the KKK is going directly against the commands of Jesus. The coexist belief is a farce because the Quran would then call for the annihilation of Christians, Jews, homosexuals, pacifists, or any other people group that is not in line with Islam. I will quote directly from the Quran, which states in Surah Al-Baqarah 2:191–193,

> And kill them wherever you overtake them and expel them from wherever they have expelled you, and fitnah is worse than killing. And do not fight them at al-masjid al-Haram until they fight you there. If they fight you, then kill them. Such is the recompense of the disbelievers.

This is only one verse out of many in support of genocide and religious intolerance. There is a large push to increase exposure to religious ideologies such as that celebrated through Islam and an even larger push to remove the Christian voice. You see this occurring more frequently in schools as diversity includes everything except for Christianity because it is believed this was the predominant belief of the forefathers (which we discussed in an earlier chapter were actually deists). In an effort to increase diversity and inclusion, Christian representation has practically disappeared.

The Christian faith is the only belief system that can bring true, lasting inner transformation. This is because we need to become born again in Spirit. This can only be done through Jesus Christ when we become a new creation. This is not the same thing as temporary change or behavior modification. It is the only belief system that shows God reaching out to humanity. All religion has created is works-based salvation in which man is searching for God. The Buddhism is trying to free their soul of bad karmic energy to reach Nirvana. The Hindu is trying to return to Brahman by also working off bad karma. The Muslim hopes that they will have done enough good deeds to be seen as worthy in the eyes of Allah on the day of judgment. Salvation for a Christian is made possible by faith alone in Jesus Christ. Ephesians 2:8 (NKJV) kindly explains, "For by grace you have been saved through faith, and that not of yourselves; it is the gift of God, not of works, lest anyone should boast." It is only through the Savior that we receive the gift of the Holy Spirit, which guides us and enables us to live out the Christian life. The ability to do so on your own by following rules in order to change your behavior is not what a relationship with God is all about. It is not you doing the work, but the Holy Spirit doing the work through you. We are transformed into the character of Christ, and we grow in spiritual maturity. As a kid, I remember these bracelets that said W. W. J. D., which stood for "What would Jesus do?" We should make those the new popular trend! Are you in a tough situation? What would Jesus do?

In order to reach people for the kingdom, we have to shift our focus. Instead of putting our energy into making known the things that make us different, we should look at what makes us human. Every human craves love. Every human has broken God's law. Each of us, regardless of background, race, belief, or sexuality, falls short of the glory of God. It is the transformative power of God's love that enables us to forsake our sin. It is the promise of the new covenant that assures us that God is committed to our growth. It is praising God for a changed heart that wants to please Him. We are not called to condemn others but to show them the love of Jesus and the transformative power of the gospel. In one of Paul's letters to the church in Corinth, he writes, "What have I to do with judging those also who are outside [the church]? Do you not judge those who are inside?" (1 Corinthians 5:12, NKJV). God is the judge of the unbeliever, but we have to start by examining the conditions of our own hearts and focusing on our own walk with the Father. The love of Jesus will do the rest in transforming those outside of the church.

True understanding of diversity comes with the knowledge that not one of us is worthy of salvation. Social status, race, culture, lifestyle choice, and past mistakes are not a factor. In the eyes of God, we have all fallen, and we are all in need of His saving grace. We need to show that same kind of compassion to those who have not yet come to the knowledge of Jesus Christ. While the result of coexist is actually in opposition to its goals, the Christian faith brings true unity and peace. Nobody is better than the next person; in fact, many religions, including apostate Christianity, which is separate from the faith, have been used for political gain. Particularly true with Hinduism and the caste system. If you were poor in India, it was because you deserved it. You were born that way because of your bad karma. While the Christian faith puts everyone on the same playing field. One of the most humbling verses in the Bible has to be Galatians 6:3 (NKJV), which states, "For if anyone thinks himself to be something, when he is nothing, he deceives himself." It does not matter who you are, where you're from, what you look like, how much money you have, the cars you drive, the clothes you wear, or what others have given you praise over. We are all on the path to destruction without Jesus Christ. As a disciple of Christ, you are called to show the world the love of God.[24] Be honest about the faith and the consequences of sin in our lives, preach the good news, and stand back to allow God to do the rest. Salvation is for all people.[25]

I have found that it is important to challenge what you believe. Don't just believe something because you feel like you have to believe it. God wants us to search Him out for ourselves. Your beliefs will be tested during this time. The foundational truths of what you believe will be shaken if not firmly rooted. When we use these conversations to test the foundations of our faith, we can only grow stronger. If you are not prepared for these conversations, your faith can and will be broken. It is good to have a general understanding of the beliefs of other people. You don't have to go into great detail concerning the study of other faiths, but it is good to approach others with a bit of knowledge concerning where they stand. This shows a level of care and respect by making an effort to understand the person directly in front of you. Nobody wants to talk to someone who acts like they know it all and doesn't care about what others have to say.

The last piece of advice I would like to offer in this area is to simply talk to people about their experiences. I have learned that most people have their own idea about what it means to be a Christian based on interactions with the Christian community, both good and bad. It is a good practice to listen to others and show them that you care about what they have to say. Ask God to give you the right words in response. Study the way that Jesus spoke to the lost. If we replicate this in our daily interactions, people will be willing to listen. Do not become defensive and cut people off when they are expressing concerns about the faith. If someone is hurt or offended by something that was said, seek forgiveness and meet them with compassion. This will show the love, mercy, and grace of God. Remember that you cannot change people, only the power of God's love can transform a wounded heart. We are simply called to plant and water the seeds of the gospel, and God makes it grow. Paul explains this concept to the church in Corinth in 1 Corinthians 3:6 (NKJV), "I planted, Apollos watered, but God gave the increase." When you do this, God will work to transform the hearts of those who do not believe.

I spoke to a classmate who came from a Jewish background. When asking her what she thought about the values she learned growing up in comparison to the liberal curriculum, she admitted that she came into agreement with her professors simply to get an A. I argued that it seemed largely unfair to have to agree with the way your professor thinks and that you are not able to freely discuss a more morally traditional view on these topics. In fact, the liberal view is really the only accepted view, at the very least on a social level. Major topics that you will encounter include but are not limited to feminism, LGBTQ+, Marxism, Critical Race Theory, and different religious perspectives. Within each topic, you have other heavily debated subtopics such as abortion, socialist reform, sexual identity, white privilege, patriarchal society, etc. It is important to find a way to balance the accepted view on some of these major social issues while also sharpening our understanding of these issues from the viewpoint of our faith.

## The Mantra of Many Paths

As you encounter new beliefs and the people who hold them, you will surely hear this tossed around. There are many paths to God. I ran into this idea often, and it is extremely popular amongst believers of the New Age. As a college student, I would say, "I'm spiritual and not religious." This was probably one of my favorite things to say when asked what I believed. It was a way of being able to hold on to my beliefs and the spiritual nature of things without having to confront sin in my life. I was able to live any lifestyle that I wanted without thinking about the consequences. I thought that we were all simply spiritual beings in search of the truth. I was on to something, yet I had fallen into deception. I understand wanting to be spiritual but not religious. We look at what religion has been responsible for in this world, and it is an absolutely valid desire. The problem is that religion is man-made. Jesus Christ came to establish a working relationship between the Father and us, not to establish a new form of religion. The next idea that goes along with this belief is that life offers many paths to the same destiny. As if we are all moving toward this greater consciousness or higher form of self. This cannot be further from the truth. There is no guarantee that your path and my path will lead to the same place. I have included this idea in this chapter because of the nature of liberal (free) thought concerning diversity. The idea is that you speak your truth, and I will speak my truth. I want you to think about this in a practical way. Imagine we are sitting down together, looking at a map, deciding which road to take for a night out at a restaurant. We see two roads that we can take from our current location. We can call them roads A and B. There is no guarantee that road A and road B will lead to the same place. Road A might take us to the restaurant, but road B takes you to the next town. The only way to get to the restaurant is to turn around on road B and begin to take road A. I personally am not willing to risk my eternity traveling down road B when road A is a guarantee. In the event that I'm wrong about my faith, well, I have nothing to lose. If someone does not believe in God or eternity, and it happens to be the truth, well, they have everything to lose.

## LGBTQ+ and Christianity

For even their women exchanged the natural use for what is against nature. Likewise also the men, leaving the natural use of the woman, burned in their lust for one another.

Romans 1:26–27 (NKJV)

In an effort to increase representation, schools are including more book titles geared toward celebrating the LGBTQ+ community. This topic isn't off-limits to children or even babies. In fact, it seems that much of what is learned around this topic is taking place early on, as fifteen percent of same-sex households have at least one child under eighteen, according to the United States government's 2019 census records. In more recent years, there have even been partnerships between public libraries and drag queens for events known as Drag Queen Story Hour. There are books, movies, television shows, and even celebrities of a younger generation announcing early on that they identify as lesbian, gay, bisexual, or even transgender. When I taught eighth grade, around 40 percent of the girls claimed to be bisexual. The flood gates of openly admitting homosexuality really swung wide around 2015, when gay marriage was legalized on a federal level in the Supreme Court case of Obergefell v. Hodges. This is a topic that many churches are not equipped to handle accurately.

Perhaps one of the most shocking things is the confusion faced by children around transgenderism. Many school districts have made moves to create transgender bathrooms and are careful to use the correct pronoun by which a person wants to be identified. I had a female student who was not transgender but preferred to be referred to as he/him. There are even debates around allowing transgender athletes to play with the opposite sex, which would place other players at a disadvantage due to biological differences. Transgender adults account for less than one percent of the population in every state. The highest concentration of transgender adults at 2.7 percent is in the District of Columbia. The statistics were taken in 2016, but I would imagine they may have escalated since the increase in media attention. The media has blasted this topic, and major television stations even created shows about it. It all seems like a lot of fuss for such a low percentage of the population. I believe a lot of this is used to directly influence young impressionable minds.

One of my best friends in high school struggled with his sexuality. He was confused, scared, and had no idea how to deal with what he was feeling. He was a great friend, in fact, one of my best friends. He would often share that he felt rejected by girls and thought he wasn't attractive. He believed that no girl could love him. I asked if he had kissed a girl before. He told me he hadn't and didn't think he ever would. We walked home from school together one day, but the conversation was too deep to stop there. We went to my house, I made a snack, and we talked. We were sixteen, and he hadn't come out yet. He asked me, "If I'm gay do you think I'll go to hell?" This question was prompted by the fact that we went to a Catholic high school. Our religion teacher was gay, and although he didn't say it, everybody knew. When this topic came up in class, he said it's fine to be gay, but you can't act out your desires. This was confusing for a lot of us because it was rumored that he lived with his partner. I grew up in more of a Charismatic environment, and although I wasn't going to church at the time, he felt like I was a good person to ask. My response was, "I don't know; the Bible says yes, but if God loves, I can't see why He would send you to hell." Neither one of us knew the right answer.

Eight years later, I came to know Jesus Christ, and it was placed on my heart to make right what happened in that basement. It wasn't easy to approach him about my error, but it was something I had to do. I told him that I love him, I care about him, and because of that, I need to share what God has revealed to me. The Bible does state that homosexuality is a sin. What we need to realize is that fornication, masturbation, and even looking at someone with sexual intent (that is not your spouse) is a sin, whether in a hetero or homosexual relationship. God created us to enjoy sex within the context of marriage. It is a beautiful way for two souls to come together and become one spiritually. Our society has reduced sex to an object of power, status, and numbers. When we engage in sexual activity outside of marriage, not only does this negatively impact our ability to be truly intimate and vulnerable with our spouses later on, but we spiritually become connected to that person. All of their spiritual mess becomes your spiritual mess. The Bible views homosexuality as inordinate affection, meaning it goes against the natural order of affection intended for a heterosexual relationship as per the design of God, which fosters procreation. The Bible commands Adam and

Eve to go and be fruitful, to multiply over the face of the earth. This is not a possibility within a homosexual relationship. From a biblical standpoint, Eve was taken from Adam. In fact, the word Adam really means mankind, and many Hebrew scholars believe that the separation of Eve from Adam was more like splitting mankind in half. This is why the Bible teaches that, in marriage, two become one flesh. When man and woman come together, there is almost a completion as one compliments the other. In many heterosexual relationships, men and women can lose themselves in the relationship and take on a new identity as a result. This is often the case for many who identify as homosexual.

One of the basic mantras of the LGBTQ+ community is that they were born that way. To which I would say, yes, we are all born with a flesh nature. Galatians 5:19 lists the works of the flesh, and the first work listed is that of sexual immorality. When we engage in sexual activity outside of God's design for intimate relationships and the covenant of marriage, then we are engaging in sexually immoral behavior and only satisfying our flesh nature. The belief that you are born gay is a way of marrying your identity to your sexual preference. A core belief of Christians is that our identity is not constructed by what we do. In other words, we are not our actions. This is a powerful revelation to grasp. You are not defined by your successes or failures. A Christian believes that their identity is in Christ as a child of God. It is the position of knowing you are a son or daughter of God that defines your purpose, motivation for life, and other things that make up the fullness of human aspiration. A well-known Christian spoken word artist, Jackie Hill Perry, who formerly identified as a lesbian, is now married to a man. She has said that lesbianism is an identity that she used to walk in and actively chose, but now she does not.

Another very powerful testimony is that of Rosaria Butterfield. She is a former women's studies professor at Syracuse University. As a result of being influenced by feminist philosophy, Butterfield adopted a lesbian identity in her twenties. She became a Christian in 1999, and she believes that how she feels does not define who she is. Love is defined differently for Christians. Although sexual touch and feelings of attraction are an expression of eros love, there is more that defines this abstract concept. Love for a Christian is a choice. We choose to love regardless of how we feel. Feelings are fleeting and do not necessarily define the true reality or nature of something. The Bible records the greatest demonstration of love as Christ dying on the cross. Nothing attractive about nails in your hands and thorns on your head. There is nothing attractive about the cross. It was pain and not pleasure. Yet this was the greatest demonstration of love. When you have a child, there is a love that fills you before the child has had a chance to ever do anything for you. What if our love for that child was defined by what they do? We would then attribute poor behavior to their identity. We might attribute good behavior to their identity as well. This shows a very conditional love that opposes the love of God, which is without conditions. We should not define a person's identity simply by their actions or attractions.

The concept of being born gay came from Freud, who we mentioned earlier was a humanist. He believed that human personality consisted of the id, ego, and superego. The id is the most primal part of our personality, and it is present from birth. The id seeks pleasure and demands to have its desires satisfied. This also includes sexual desires as present from birth. Freud discusses five stages of psycho-sexual development, believing that sexual energy (libido) manifests in different areas at different ages but mostly between zero and five years old. This is where the idea of being born homosexual was really birthed. Freud is one of the leading psychologists discussed in schools today. It is important to understand how his theories are driving thought around the development of sexuality. Unfortunately, a basic psychology class only takes you so far and usually unpacks the teachings of other humanists. Heinz Kohut, on the other hand, rejected the teachings of Freud and developed a different theory of defining the self. He believed that a person was impacted by their childhood upbringing and that the self was developed through unmet or met needs as a direct result of empathy given or not given by early caregivers and parents. One unmet need that many face in childhood is acceptance.

The LGBTQ+ community offers a very strong sense of community. People feel like they are with those who understand and accept them. Isn't that what we all want? A sense of feeling loved, accepted, and understood? The first identity marker that is often proudly stated is gay. Although the community offers fellowship and acceptance, it actually reduces the value of the individual to being marked by their sexual orientation.

The truth is that those who identify as gay are much more than that. They have a purpose, they are loved, they are accepted, and Christ died for them too. For those of you reading this who identify as homosexual, I want to ask you something. Are you not much more than your sexual preference? This is why I stressed the importance of knowing who you are in Christ. If you are unsure of your identity, then you will become anything another person says that you are. This was true for me. I was a chameleon. I could be whatever you wanted me to be as long as I was accepted. This was also the case with my friend. He was bullied in school, and people always said that they thought he was gay. He sort of took on this identity as he did not know who he was. He felt peer pressure from others and constant rejection from girls. All of these things led to a place of sadness, isolation, and confusion. Nobody wants to stay in that place. The good news is that you don't have to stay there. You can come into truly knowing who you are as you come to know the Father in heaven.

Many church leaders and goers will tell you that homosexuality is a choice and you can just get over it. This is an insensitive approach to a very sensitive issue. There are plenty of people who struggle with these feelings, and as a result, there is a high suicide rate for transgender and other LGBTQ+ community members. For many, it began with unwanted feelings and sexual urges that began with much confusion. In some cases, after several failed or traumatic relationships with the opposite sex, the desire for inordinate affection took precedence. In other cases, it has been reported that homosexual desires took place after experiencing molestation by someone of the same sex at a young age. Whatever the situation, we need to be sensitive to hear the hearts of those around us so that we might be able to introduce the love of Jesus. In fact, I love the story of Rosaria Butterfield, who stated in an interview that when she came to know Jesus, homosexuality was not even the first thing in which she was convicted. That conviction came later. She goes on to discuss that a pastor who approached her with grace and love by extending a hand of friendship is what led her to ask questions. It was not the judgmental nature that many in this community have been met with when confronted concerning their sexuality. I am sad to say that my friend from high school stopped speaking to me after I told him my stance. I asked God if there was another way. How could I prevent that same thing from happening again and reach this community for You? God made something very clear to me when I asked that question. He reminded me that my role as His disciple is to introduce others to Him. To guide them into a relationship with Him by being His witness. As I would testify to others about the good things God has done in my life, their curiosity would peak. Once that person came into a relationship with God, the Holy Spirit would bring conviction to the sin areas present in the new believer's life. The same is true for you. Be a friend. Reflect the love of Christ. Introduce them to Him. He will reveal their identity and live through them.

## Feminism and Christianity

Nevertheless, neither is man independent of woman, nor woman independent of man, in the Lord. For as woman came from man, even so man also comes through woman; but all things are from God.

1 Corinthians 11:11–12 (NKJV)

Feminism has had several faces over the years. In some cases being a feminist was about a woman being made equal to a man. Equality for the feminist was often represented through symbols of status such as career advancements. Some view feminism now as a way of empowering a woman to be above a man and treating males as if they are lesser. Our education system celebrates feminism by honoring women's history month and bringing female writers, activists, scientists, and other prominent figures into the spotlight. There is nothing wrong with celebrating the achievements of incredible women. However, the message behind modern feminism is really the problem. One of which relies on the fact that men are oppressors and Christian men are the epitome of oppressive patriarchy. Modern feminism is attractive to students for a multitude of reasons.

Picture this scenario. It's 1955; the nation is segregated; men head off to work from their picturesque suburban home while a well-kept woman remains home, keeps the house perfect, cares for the children, and has a nice hot meal ready for the table each night. You may have pictured something like the 1957 sitcom series *Leave It to*

*Beaver*. This is the picture often sold as the American dream. It makes sense that this image has become deeply ingrained in the American psyche, with the skyrocketing of television sales from around 6,000 in 1946 to 12 million by 1951. This image was reinforced by centuries of patriarchal societies. We learn that women were not allowed to vote, they were forced to care for their children, and there were no opportunities for them to go to school or make a meaningful career. It is from this line of thinking that systemic oppression is highlighted, spotlighting terms like the glass ceiling and gender wage gap. Don't get me wrong; there is nothing wrong with wanting to see equal pay for equal work. The problem lies in the mindset of American values. Our society equates economic status with success. Our economic status is tied to our choice of career, and staying at home doesn't pay. This creates two issues. Firstly, being a mother and caring for children is seen as oppressive, and women should be like men or even above them. Oftentimes, the Bible will be used as a reference in order to reinforce this image. This has led to an overall rejection of the Bible in the areas concerning male and female roles. In the name of equality, our society has rejected some basic truths, including the way that the Bible views women.

Perhaps one of the greatest misconceptions concerning women from a biblical worldview is differentiating between God's heart and religion. God has always viewed women as precious creations and certainly not second-class citizens. In fact, when God created Eve, the Bible states that Adam needed a companion that was comparable to him (Genesis 2:18). This meant that all of what God had created prior to the creation of Eve was not equal to Adam. Another important thing to understand is that God has worked through many women. In fact, several women were used as part of God's plan to save Israel. At no point does God condone the mistreatment of women or behavior that is controlling. In fact, the Bible tells us that a husband's prayers can be hindered depending on how he treats his wife (1 Peter 3:7). There have been many examples throughout history of toxic masculinity or what the Latinx community refers to as machismo men. That behavior is more in line with the religious spirit. A good example of this is when the Pharisees (a sect of Jews during Jesus' time) brought a woman who was found caught in the act of adultery to be stoned. Jesus knew their hearts and famously said, "He that is without sin among you, let him first cast a stone at her" (John 8:7, KJV). That is a powerful representation of men and women being on equal footing before God. We all have sinned and fallen short of the glory of God. Jesus actually touched on the treatment of women several times and continued this work through Paul. Colossians 3:19 (BLB) states, "Husbands, love your wives and do not be harsh toward them." God is deeply concerned with how women are treated. To take this a step forward, Jesus also knew that the Pharisees were corrupt. The law actually stated that if a case of adultery was found out that both the man and the woman should be brought to trial. In this case, only the woman was brought. Jesus needed to deal with the deep corruption of His Word as it was displayed by religious people. I don't think much has really changed in this regard.

An entire book could be dedicated to women in the Bible; in fact, there are many books that touch on this topic. I want to show you the way in which God truly sees a woman. For those of you who are women or young girls reading this book, let this scripture be your aspiration. For the men or young men reading this book, let this be the woman you pursue. Proverbs 31 highlights some major insights about a godly woman. Proverbs 31:10 (NKJV) states, "Who can find a virtuous wife? For her worth is far above rubies." A godly woman is highly valuable. Remember that thing about women not working? The Bible disagrees. Not only does she work with her hands (Proverbs 31:13, NKJV), but she prepares food for her household. Did I also mention that she is a businesswoman? Proverbs 31:16 (NKJV), "She considers a field and buys it; From her profits she plants a vineyard." She also "makes linen garments and sells them, And supplies sashes for the merchants" (Proverbs 31:24, NKJV). She takes care of the poor (Proverbs 31:20) and makes sure her house is in order (Proverbs 31:21). Do you know that saying that behind every powerful man is a powerful woman? Well, the Bible agrees and states that women have the power to either build up or destroy a nation. This is done primarily through influence. The influence of a godly woman greatly impacts her husband, who because of her is "known in the gates, When he sits among the elders of the land" (Proverbs 31:23, NKJV). The Bible says she is strong and honored as these are the garments she wears (Proverbs 31:25). A virtuous woman is wise and kind (Proverbs 31:26). All while caring for and raising up her children (Proverbs 31:28). To sum it all up, she is basically a superwoman! This is true women's empowerment. Being a strong woman does not mean being someone's slave or trying to be like a man.

One way to view the issues around male and female differences includes the belief that men are stronger than women and that women are too sensitive. We must realize that men and women are different. They were designed to function differently. Regardless of the differences, there are some truths that must be understood. Biological and hormonal differences are present at birth. Even the structure found inside the nucleus of a cell differs. Males have an XY chromosome, and females have XX. Biologically, boys have more testosterone which encourages the growth of tissues and aids in building muscle. Girls produce estrogen, which is primarily responsible for regulating the menstrual cycle and other biological markers. In some women, the increase and decrease of estrogen can impact the levels of serotonin which is responsible for regulating anxiety, happiness, and mood. Although men are biologically stronger than women because of their ability to produce muscles in a different way, women are certainly not weak. Women produce more estrogen and are open to cyclical hormonal changes, but that does not mean that they are emotionally unstable or unfit to ever make decisions. Different does not mean unequal.

Relationship dynamics must also be addressed. We were created to work together within a given relationship. There are some things that women are just naturally better at doing, and the same goes for men. Although the examples I will give are not always the case, it is the general pattern. Men and women were designed to use their

God-given strengths to work cooperatively together. Men have been given this capacity to lead in a home by making agreed-upon and sacrificial decisions. When this is out of balance, men have a tendency to become passive about certain issues while the woman assumes double the household responsibility. There needs to be a balance in the home. Women, on the other hand, have been given a natural ability to love and nurture children through which their own body has nourished and grown. The 1950s image of the family can be destructive when a father is more involved with work than in the life of his children. Parenting is a partnership. Chores are a partnership. Finances are a partnership. A true way to see a successful marriage is to remain as partners. Although partnership is necessary, there is a natural bond between a mother and her child that is essential for the child's growth. When a baby is born, they are instantly placed on their mother's chest for skin-to-skin contact. Without the love of bonding, a child can end up having problems with attachment in the future. Mother is not equal to burden. It is a beautiful privilege to bear and rear children. When we stigmatize the title mother, we view having children as a burden instead of a joy. In fact, Deborah is a great biblical example of a strong woman who was raised up to lead and deliver Israel in a time of war. Not much is mentioned about her husband, other than the fact that it is believed that she was married. It is believed that she didn't have any children of her own. Yet even with her impressive military strategies, she is remembered as being a mother to Israel. She is a great example of the fact that you can not only do something amazing in the world but can wear the title of mother too. Motherhood is not an easy task. The responsibility of raising up the future generation is no small thing.

What if I told you that modern feminism is partly responsible for the way we see the home broken apart today? Many families have two parents working full-time jobs. That's at least forty hours a week for each parent. In many cases, it means a single-parent household with shared visitation and more than one job. Children are not getting the time and support they need to be truly nurtured. They are being raised by television programs and the education system. The same system that this book has explained begins teaching much of the anti-God rhetoric and humanist beliefs from preschool through college. We can see the attack on the family as other things fight for our daily attention. Strong families have the ability to impact the world. There has even been a direct correlation between dysfunctional family dynamics and crime. Family is God's design, and it is meant to display the desire that God has to see His children come home and know Him as Father. What was so appealing about that 1950s picture of the family? It is the classic picture of smiling faces sitting around a family table. Family time now is very rare. The United States faces a divorce rate of nearly 50 percent. Many families have given their attention to their tablets, smart devices, jobs, after-school activities, and other things. How many people actually sit together for a family meal? We have pushed God and His design for family out of the equation. This is not to say that the 1950s picture of the family is totally realistic, but rather that it displays an ideal. A longing that is placed in each heart for familial closeness.

Before I came into a deeper relationship with God, I was highly supportive of many feminist teachings. I believed that Christians oppressed women and that I would never be able to lead, although I felt a natural call to leadership. As a kid, I would take charge and be the first one to come up with a plan during recess games. I played sports and would inspire and encourage my fellow teammates to win. One of the things that turned me away from the Christian faith was a misunderstanding about leadership as a woman. I thought that following Christ meant that I was going to be oppressed, and I was never allowed to lead anything. This is so far from the truth. I have been given the ability in Christ to lead others to the truth. There are a lot of young people out there that are hurting, searching for fulfillment, and in need of guidance. Let's discuss the leadership of women a little further. A common lie that has been told to young girls is that Christianity does not align with any examples of female leadership. The Bible recounts stories in which God has used women in such a big way. I will go as far as to say that Christ is the vindicator of women. If you read the book of Judges, you will find that God raised Deborah to be a leader of the Israelites. Queen Esther saw her people saved by going boldly before the king. Ruth showed her dedication to Naomi in the book of Ruth, and God rewarded her. Jesus Christ came from Mary, a woman who was highly favored in the sight of God. Priscilla was most likely an elder used in spreading the message of the gospel in the early church. The apostle Paul addresses many women as being those who labored to spread the good news of Jesus Christ.[26] Jesus appeared to a woman first after His crucifixion.

There are countless examples of women being healed by displaying great faith. I struggled with the concept of female oppression and Christianity for a long time. A twisted view of Christianity presented through feminism only added fuel to the fire. Fortunately, I have arrived at the truth. Jesus has a great love for women. Our God is amazing and does not condone treating women poorly, talking down to them, or making them inferior. As we discussed previously, women are to be loved, cared for, and cherished.

There are plenty of other examples of how God used women to do amazing things in the Bible; it is certainly something worth exploring further. We have to remember the true enemy of the woman, and it is not the man. It is none other than Satan. God placed hatred between the woman and the serpent because of the evil that was committed on the day on which Adam and Eve fell into sin due to disobedience to God. The enemy knew that the Savior would be brought into the earth through a woman. He also hates the fact that more babies are brought into the earth through women who are created in God's image. Genesis 3:15 (NKJV), "And I will put enmity Between you and the woman, And between your seed and her Seed; He shall bruise your head, And you shall bruise His heel." When Jesus Christ came and won the victory over death and hell, Satan lost his power to rule over those born again in Christ. Why is this important? Because we need to identify the one who truly hates women, the enemy of your soul. The one who truly desires to enslave women is none other than the serpent himself. Our common enemy understands the influence of a woman. The Bible discusses both righteous and wicked women.

Proverbs goes as far as to mention that a wicked woman has the ability to destroy kings (31:3). This is the power of influence. Women have the ability to either build or destroy a kingdom.

In some cases, modern feminism goes beyond equality into demeaning men. It says that you have to be like a man in order to be equal to him. Remember, different roles lead to a relationship that is able to function properly. It is kind of like a magnet. If you have two positives or two negatives, the ends of the magnet will refuse to stick together. Though they are different, a positive and negative magnet will stick closely together. The same is true for a husband and wife. This joining together is beautifully reflected in Genesis 2:24 (NKJV), "Therefore a man shall leave his father and mother and be joined to his wife, and they shall become one flesh." There is a beautiful bond that takes place when a man and woman are united together in the Spirit through the promise of marriage, which is blessed by God. They are no longer viewed as two but as one. This is why divorce is so devastating to a family because God designed marriage to be a bonding experience. How can one divorce his own flesh? This does not, however, give either a man or a woman the right to demean, abuse, control, or manipulate the other. Two that become one is the definition of coming together in equality. This can't work unless both men and women are functioning within their proper roles. I'm not saying this means that the ladies should shut up and make a sandwich. This does mean that a man is to protect his house and a woman is to nurture. Ladies, there is nothing oppressive about serving and loving your husbands and children. In fact, as Christians, we are to exemplify the love of Christ, which was not only sacrificial but in service to others. The same goes for husbands. To be considered the head of the household does not mean that you can control your family. The Bible calls men to sacrifice their wants, needs, and desires for the sake of the betterment of their families. Marriage is to reflect service to each other. There is something beautiful about a marriage that functions in this way. A marriage that will lead to greater intimacy, joy, and fulfillment.

## Racism and Christianity

The stranger who dwells among you shall be to you as one born among you, and you shall love him as yourself; for you were strangers in the land of Egypt: I am the Lord your God.

Leviticus 19:34 (NKJV)

Racism is a very heavily discussed issue in the classroom. American history textbooks pinpoint racial issues in a very linear way. White Christians are predominately blamed for slavery in America and other woes of colonization.

The pushback is so strong concerning this time period that the early Protestant settlers are villainized, while natives and early African slaves are described as being exploited and unjustly treated. The way that history compartmentalizes people and circumstances has created a deep level of division in our schools. When I taught my high school and middle school students, I was able to gain a great level of respect from them. I didn't earn their respect because I acted as though I was superior to them and that they, based on skin color, were inferior to me. Although, it is sad to say that this attitude did exist and in some places still does in schools and other institutions.

The approach with my students was to treat them all equally. I saw them as human beings who had their own unique gifts and talents. As a teacher, my job was not solely for you to perform well on state tests. My role was to be a mentor. Lessons about kindness, empathy, shared understanding, and honor were much more valuable than if you understood the metaphor used in the story. I did not do this at the expense of healthy discipline. My students respected me for holding them accountable while also encouraging them to be and give their very best. I never saw skin color as a hindrance to what they were capable of accomplishing. The way that critical race theory has permeated the classroom reinforces the oppression that people of color face on a generational scale. I never felt the best approach to connecting with my students was to prime them to believe that no matter how hard they worked, the systems were against them, and they could not succeed. That's just not the truth. There are so many successful people of color who have accomplished incredible things. Victimization should never be part of that. Yet, in an effort to disrupt the traditional lineup of predominately white male figures in academia, color lines have been drawn, creating a state of division, leading to feelings of hostility and confusion amongst students and staff. When the situation with George Floyd was at its peak on national television, a friend called me. She asked me to pray for her because she felt intense fear. She had experienced a history of victimization, and this event triggered some past traumatic experiences being a woman of color. Although I have never experienced debilitating fear through a trigger like that one, I lent an ear and prayed with her. She is a Christian and understands that although people in this world do terrible things, it is not an accurate depiction of all people or of the God we both love. At that moment, her skin color played a role in the trauma she carried. All trauma brings bondage, but she understood that she was not a victim of her trauma. The color of skin that God gave you when He created you was not an accident and should never be associated predominately with traumatic experiences.

While some may say that my approach to the students is "color blind," I believe it's exactly what they need to not take on victimization as a marker of identity. Color blindness is a term used to mean that a person is denying the history of victimization experienced by people of color by taking the stance that color is not an indicator of the way that individuals should be treated or viewed. Some say that this is denying their experiences. I don't believe any experience is denied, but instead, a conscious choice is being made in which one does not need to be defined by maltreatment. The middle school that I previously worked for was highly concerned with the school-to-prison pipeline. In an effort to combat this issue, professional developments around race were held. There were two difficult experiences that I faced that reinforced the divisive behavior.

I recall one particular instance where a woman had just finished playing a video that mentioned that race is a social construct meant to bring about oppressive power dynamics. This stuck out to me because, as a Christian, I believe that we are one human race. This is true biologically and according to Scripture. All of mankind originates from the same ancestors. Even according to some modern evolutionary theories, it is believed that humans share a common ancestor. If all of humanity stems from Adam and Eve, we are all of one race. There are variations when it comes to hair color/texture, skin color based on melanin levels, and various eye colors. We are one race nonetheless. Within humanity exists variations. This includes cultural and ethnic variations. When asked to share a key takeaway from the video, I explained that race as a social construct intrigued me. I proceeded to explain that we are technically one human race and if we understood that, then perhaps there would be less division. I am not sure if the presenter watched the video, but she instantly stated that what I was pointing out was connected to color blindness and that I was showing a form of bias. Honestly, I was in shock.

The chaos of this professional development wasn't done just yet. The second presenter showed a video of white students bullying students of color. The students being bullied were black, Asian, and Hispanic. At this point, the room felt very uncomfortable because of the picture that was being painted. There were no instances of bullying displayed that showed a white student at the receiving end. This shows a high level of bias in itself. I am not saying that this doesn't or hasn't happened. I can say that based on my personal experience, including teaching and attending a Brooklyn public school, I have seen racial bullying all across the board. In fact, I have seen divisions among students of color who clash based on background. I have had African, Haitian, Caribbean, and black American students. All of which I have seen at different points both support and bully one another while bringing their cultural background into the conflict. I've also witnessed this amongst my Hispanic students who varied from South American countries, Mexico, Dominican Republic, Puerto Rico, and other places. I've seen this among my Middle Eastern students. I've seen the division amongst my European students. Hurt humans will always look to use our differences in order to play into power dynamics. Race, ethnicity, and culture are only a piece of the puzzle used to exert power over other individuals. The issues surrounding power dynamics transcend color, gender, and socio-economic status.

While attending a middle school in Brooklyn, I was bullied by a Hispanic girl and a Haitian girl. They threatened to jump me almost daily while in seventh grade. Both girls made hateful comments about me being white. The way that the issue concerning race is being taught in schools does not count this as racism. This is because of the way popular voices around critical race theory define racism. I have also experienced bullying from other white students who came from wealthier backgrounds. Oppression comes in many shapes, colors, and sizes. When humans have experienced oppression, they can themselves become oppressors. From a Christian standpoint, we are all oppressed as slaves to the flesh and in need of salvation. This in no way excuses the mistreatment of any life as all life is precious, valuable, and created in the image of God.

You might think that racism is the belief that groups of humans have different behavioral traits based on inherited characteristics leading to a division based on the superiority of one race over another. This can result in discrimination or hostility directed at a group of people viewed as inferior. Critical race theory activists do not share this common definition. Instead, they define racism as discrimination and prejudice targeting a particular group that has been historically oppressed. This means that because white people have not been historically oppressed due to the color of their skin, they cannot be considered victims of racism. This creates a greater power imbalance. The presenter of the professional development used this definition in an attempt to shame me publicly. He expressed that I could not ever experience racism because I have white privilege. I went on to ask what this means for someone like my son, whose father is Ecuadorian and has brown skin. My son is fair, like me, and I come from an Italian background. My son, in this case, would also have white privilege because he is perceived to be white. Critical race theory hinges on perception. You can identify in any way that you choose, but your advantages or disadvantages in society stem from how others perceive you. In the case of my son, his skin color gives an advantage, but his last name is Spanish, and this places him at a disadvantage, according to the theory. There are so many layers to this, and there is no intention to deny any experience. I just cannot see how this theory which has led to the support of movements like Black Lives Matter, is actually achieving its intended outcome. Better yet, it would be beneficial for such a movement to more clearly define the intended outcome, as this seems to change depending on who you ask. In an effort to understand this theory further, I then asked what would happen if my son was bullied by a white student of European descent. Would that be racism because he is half Ecuadorian but does not appear to be Hispanic? The short answer is no. In reality, your lineage does not matter. It is how others perceive you. This puts mixed folks in an awkward place because they share the history of slavery through one parent but the history of oppression through another (when the theory is applied). The point is that this all functions in circular thinking. The arguments never really create any desired result. All this does is place you on a logistical hamster wheel. Instead of creating equality, it perpetuates more inequality. To place your identity in the hands of victimhood only creates greater levels of oppressed thinking.

What was perhaps the most astonishing experience was the professional development that took place at the end of the year. The speaker was questioning the motives of white teachers. She even advocated for the re-segregation of schools. The presenter asked why we (white teachers) bothered to show up and teach our students since we didn't look like them. I am all about representation. I think it is important to see role models that truly reflect the ethnic variations that are present here on Earth. Heaven is diverse,

> After this I looked, and behold, a great multitude that no one could number, from every nation, from all tribes and peoples and languages, standing before the throne and before the Lamb, clothed in white robes, with palm branches in their hands.

> Revelation 7:9 (ESV)

While I believe that critical race theory only further divides us, we are all equal in God's eyes. We are actually advised to treat others with greater regard than even ourselves, and there is no division based on racial characteristics.[27] Several teachers were expressing frustration at the very clear level of bias. When another teacher of color spoke against what was being shared, the virtual meeting space was awkward as she was able to speak on the topic because it was her experience. However, her experience was counter-narrative and, therefore, not useful in pushing forward the agenda. Another teacher spoke out and said she was doing her very best to teach her students, but after the professional development, she didn't know what else to do and felt like she was failing the kids because her white presence in the room (according to the presenter), on its own, is harmful. The presenter went on to explain that there is no way we can understand the trauma of a person of color. The school counselor thought it would be a good idea to add that the trauma a white student experiences can never be more than a black or Hispanic student. I personally would never send my child to a school where their pain would be minimized in this way by someone who is called to be impartial. Although the woman who made the statement that white teachers should stay in white schools also stated that teachers should not be impartial but take a stand in the classroom to become anti-racist themselves. I'm all for advocating for personal rights, but that needs to be done with care and consideration for all of your students and not just some. This type of thinking creates frustration and does not offer real solutions.

These concepts are generally celebrated in the classroom with little to no context as to the message being sent. Several states have moved to ban the teaching of critical race theory for its divisive nature. My students even struggled to understand some of these concepts as they didn't see themselves as victims of past generations. This ideology is glorified through various forms of media. Books such as *How to Be an Antiracist* by Ibram X. Kendi call people not to be passive but rather action-oriented. Another book that targets babies and toddlers is *Antiracist Baby* by the same author. While many schools include race as a marker of identity, the push for inclusion also means studying material from certain groups who have expressed anti-white or pro-black rhetoric. Such as that of the Black Panther Party led by Muslim Communist Malcolm X. A popular movie and novel called *The Hate U Give* explores the divide between law enforcement and people of color. It is safe to say that conversations around race have been turbulent and what is currently being done isn't working. It is very difficult to even discuss this issue without hostility, particularly on a college campus. One specific example of this divide took place in between classes while in school for my master's degree. There had been a pro-black (her words) group on campus who was protesting the current climate between law enforcement and the community. I saw this as an opportunity to lend an ear to another student. I believe that as Christians, we are called to walk in a high level of understanding for those around us. I naïvely believed that she would be open to a conversation. When I asked why they were protesting and what they hoped would be the result, she freaked out. She went on to tell me she couldn't even look at me and insulted me with a slew of other statements. That told me everything I needed to know. The social manipulation from major media outlets only adds fire to situations like the one I described above. A 2020 NBC article was titled, "Racism among white Christians is higher than among nonreligious. That's no coincidence." Titles like this are damaging and deny the truth of the role many Christians have played in coming against racism. Titles like that are designed to play into the left-right paradigm, only further turning the general population against one another. This is part of the common narrative in which people associate white Christians with oppressors. Schools do not discuss the numerous churches that stood against slavery or those that supported the civil rights movement. Those details are often removed or overlooked because it is counterproductive to the narrative. That is a part of forgotten history. Granted, the church for slaves was often used as a resource for manipulation and twisting the Word of God to ensure a mindset of servitude. That does not mean that God didn't meet slaves where they were and be God to them. It's a classic example of the enemy (in a spiritual and physical sense) attempting to exert control over people and blame God for all of it.

It would be wrong to deny that historically there has been oppression and hatred toward people of color. The real issue is when an ideology stigmatizes one group as being the sole responsible for the oppression. Christians have almost become a scapegoat. I do not believe true followers of the faith could ever actually justify the brutal beatings, manipulation, hatred, and even murder that was experienced by American slaves, Native Americans, and other traditionally marginalized people groups. As mentioned earlier in the book, I don't believe many of the early American leaders truly had a relationship with Christ if they considered themselves to be deists. It's kind of like how the dollar bill reads, "In God We Trust."

When we know who God is to the deist or to the secular humanist, we understand that the God of the Bible is not who is being honored. The whole system of white supremacy goes further back than you might think and is not isolated to the United States. This includes Hitler's love for eugenics and the connection to preserving the Aryan race. The Aryans in many cultures were almost deified and worshipped as gods because their features were unique compared to the features of those who originated from regions in the Middle East. Aryans were typically tall, fair-skinned, and were believed to have blue eyes. The history of the Aryans and their influence on the world goes beyond the limits of what the book intends to cover. However, it is highly advised to do your own research, and you will see that this issue goes far beyond Americans, Christians, Republicans, or anybody else who acts as a scapegoat for the incredible pain faced by slaves and the after-effects on generations that followed.

Bias and stereotypes have been around for a long time. In the Bible, Jesus touches on the issue of bias. He gives a parable that transcends color, age, wealth, and status lines. The parable of "The Good Samaritan" would be a great shock to His Jewish followers. The Jews and the Samaritans had a long history, and it's safe to say they didn't really like each other very much. The parable is told in Luke 10:25–37. A lawyer asked Jesus to explain the greatest law, and He responded in verse 27 (ESV), "You shall love the Lord your God with all your heart and with all your soul and with all your strength and with all your mind, and your neighbor as yourself." We love our neighbors when we understand that they, too, were created in the image of God. When we love God, we are able to love what has been made in His image. The lawyer proceeded to ask who exactly is his neighbor. Jesus then opens up with the parable of "The Good Samaritan." He speaks about a man who was stripped of his clothes, beaten, and left for dead. As the man lay on the floor in a helpless situation, three different men passed by him. The first man was a priest. There is a form of bias here and an assumption that surely a priest would do the right thing and help out. Jesus explains that, instead, he went to the other side of the road and continued walking. Not the response we might have expected. The second was a Levite. They worked to maintain the temple, sang praises, and did other religious acts. Surely, the Levite would help the man. The Levite responded the same way as the priest and passed the man by crossing to the other side of the road. Finally, a Samaritan comes along. Not only did the Samaritan bandage the man's wounds, pour oil and wine, and set him on his own animal, but he went the extra mile. He brought the man to an innkeeper and paid for his stay. He even offered to pay more if the man accrued additional expenses. Jesus was trying to show us that things aren't always as they appear. We should not judge based on the outward appearance of things. Even that which seems religious may not reflect the heart of God in loving those around us. If we treat any group as inferior to ourselves, we are certainly not acting in love. The Jews hated the Samaritans, called them half-breeds, and would rather cross the Jordan River than travel through Samaria. Jesus knew that this was a problem, and we can apply this parable to racial tensions present today. This parable truly reflects how God's heart feels toward issues such as hatred, bias, and oppression.

No true Christian would be comfortable seeing others mistreated or enslaved. This is contrary to what Christ taught His disciples. I have heard it often argued that the Bible supports slavery. This is not true. Slavery has been around for thousands of years. It was a common practice to enslave the inhabitants of conquered lands, and there were many examples of prejudice or outright bias. The Old Testament laws refer to ways in which a slave should be treated. God's design was not for slaves to be present in the world, but rather humans are agents of free will, and so the Bible offers ways in which to handle such situations around a common practice of the time period. The Bible also paints a vivid picture of servitude. First Corinthians 7:22 explains that we are servants of Christ. Some versions use slave instead of servant. The Greek uses the word *doulos* to mean one who is devoted to another in disregard of one's own interests. Christians believe that we are to be fully surrendered or submitted to God so that He may work in and through us. The Bible uses this as a metaphor to explain our spiritual condition before God. It goes on to explain that we are slaves to sin because of the corrupted nature of the flesh. It's the urge to do wrong things that drives us unless it is crucified, and we walk in the power of the Holy Spirit, which enables us to live a life turning away from sin, which, left to its own devices, produces death. The good news is that Jesus can deliver us from being slaves to our sinful nature. Not only does God deliver us, but He frees us from fear and death. Regardless of racial, cultural, or social status, we know two facts: we have all been born, and we will all die. The devil uses fear to keep us in bondage. I remember being in class and discussing whether it was better to be a leader who is loved or one who is feared. Interestingly, fear motivates us to act in a way of self-preservation, while love motivates us to give of ourselves. Love enables us to willfully submit ourselves before one another in service to them. This is the vast difference between serving the world and serving Christ. God is so loving and merciful toward us that those who have been forgiven of much cling tightly to Him and desire to serve Him faithfully.[28] We see a recurring theme in the Bible of God pouring out His love on a world that has been lost and broken. When we come to understand God's great love and mercy, we desire to serve Him. It is kind of like when your parents, grandparents, or respected authority figure says, "I am disappointed in you." Those are the words that pierce through to the soul because we know in their love we were free to make the right choice, and we made the wrong one instead. When a parent screams at us or maybe hits us, the reaction is no longer one of love but of fear which leads to self-preservation and feelings of bondage.

Fear is how the enemy can motivate us to act in ways we shouldn't. Perhaps your financial situation isn't good, and you fear being out on the street, so you steal from somebody. Perhaps you got pregnant out of wedlock and secretly had an abortion out of fear of not being able to care for the child. Perhaps you didn't study for that final exam and cheated in fear of losing the scholarship to the school you couldn't otherwise afford. There are many reasons why we do things we shouldn't. Instead of living in fear, condemnation, and guilt, we must find the strength and humility to come to Christ and receive His love, mercy, and forgiveness. It is only God's perfect love that can cast out fear.[29] Fear has no place in the lives of God's children. There is no need for us to live under self-preservation. God promised to fight for us and was crucified to release us from the bondage that fear brings. A Christian who truly trusts God can go through the worst type of hell on Earth and still believe that God is in control. This means that nothing can hurt you. That is true freedom from all fear, including death, both spiritual and physical.[30] That type of freedom is available to all people.

## Back to the Garden

Then the Lord God took the man and put him in the garden of Eden to tend and keep it.

Genesis 2:15 (NKJV)

Racism, feminism, LGBTQ+, and other hot-button topics are sure to spring up as social learning is an increasingly large portion of many education curriculums. No matter the topic or the issues surrounding them, it all comes down to one thing: the human condition. God has an incredible way of essentially laying a breadcrumb trail for us to follow so that we can walk powerfully into our God-given purpose. The breadcrumb trail for me began with an intense curiosity to better understand the story of creation. God has given me the gift of connection, and so I naturally was curious to know how various cultures around the world also viewed the creation story. This line of questioning and studying led me to collect the information I needed, but something was still missing. I remember preparing to submit my thesis paper in college. The professor assigned to my thesis was perhaps one of my favorite professors, and he was a religious man. We didn't call him professor or mister, but he was referred to as brother. I asked him a very heartfelt question. I asked him how he maintained faith in God while being exposed to so much anti-Christian literature and philosophical thought. He simply told me that he didn't let the two things mix together. While I believe his answer was genuine, it didn't quite offer the fulfillment I was seeking. How can they not be mixed together? Surely there were lenses through which the world was painted for the various authors. How did they get those lenses? The nagging question still remained in my research. How was it possible that many societies, removed by time and space, had some form of creation story? They had not mentioned evolution but creation. I have never believed that ancient cultures were as far behind as we are taught. In fact, it was the Egyptians who regularly practiced surgery. Many of these societies knew much more about humanity than our modern history textbook would like to teach. I recognized that something extremely important about humanity could be revealed through these stories, and I was determined to uncover it. It wasn't until I encountered the Lord in February of 2018 that the missing puzzle piece was found. God took me on a journey of understanding much of what I wanted to know about the human condition, creation, and the fall of mankind, as mentioned in the book of Genesis. This book is key for us to know who we are, how we function, and the necessity of Jesus' death on the cross.

Genesis 3:1–10 of the New King James Version reads:

> Now the serpent was more cunning than any beast of the field which the Lord God had made. And he said to the woman, "Has God indeed said, 'You shall not eat of every tree of the garden'?" And the woman said to the serpent, "We may eat the fruit of the trees of the garden; but of the fruit of the tree which is in the midst of the garden, God has said, 'You shall not eat it, nor shall you touch it, lest you die.'" Then the serpent said to the woman, "You

will not surely die. For God knows that in the day you eat of it your eyes will be opened, and you will be like God, knowing good and evil." So when the woman saw that the tree was good for food, that it was pleasant to the eyes, and a tree desirable to make one wise, she took of its fruit and ate. She also gave to her husband with her, and he ate. Then the eyes of both of them were opened, and they knew that they were naked; and they sewed fig leaves together and made themselves coverings. And they heard the sound of the Lord God walking in the garden in the cool of the day, and Adam and his wife hid themselves from the presence of the Lord God among the trees of the garden. Then the Lord God called Adam and said to him, "Where are you?" So he said, "I heard Your voice in the garden, and I was afraid because I was naked; and I hid myself."

## Disobedience and Destruction

"We may eat the fruit of the trees of the garden; but of the fruit of the tree which is in the midst of the garden, God has said, 'You shall not eat it, nor shall you touch it, lest you die.'" Then the serpent said to the woman, "You will not surely die. For God knows that in the day you eat of it your eyes will be opened, and you will be like God, knowing good and evil."

Genesis 3:2–5 (NKJV)

There is so much that we can understand about ourselves in those verses from the Bible. We see that mankind fell due to disobedience to God. This does not imply that God is a tyrant who demands obedience. This means that without obedience to God, we walk after sin, and sin leads to spiritual death. Adam and Eve were told not to eat of the tree of knowledge of good and evil. To the modern progressive thinker, this seems like God is trying to hide something. Perhaps God does not want them to be free thinkers liberated from His dictatorship. This is a core belief of the thinkers of the Enlightenment Era. This is one of the greatest separations from God on a societal level. This is also where science became God's replacement. That's what I used to believe. That knowing God was oppressive, boring, and restrictive. That the world had so much more to offer, and there was more to discover. This cannot be further from the truth. When man disobeyed God, the decision was made to rebel from a holy, loving, all-good, and all-knowing Father. From the Creator who knows how the world functions, how you function, and your purpose. Yet here we are, like rebellious teenagers believing we have all of the answers with our limited capacity for the deep complexities of creation. We have decided to become agents of our own destiny, charting our own course, blindly stumbling through life, and wondering what will come next. We should instead choose to seek God, who gifted us, formed us, and knows why we were created.

In our rebellion, we sinned against God and began to obey our own will and desires of the flesh. This is living the kind of lifestyle that says, "I don't need God." In reality, we all need God, and it is the deceitfulness of our hearts that tell us otherwise.[31] As humans, we are unable to truly know what will lie ahead in our lives, and our hearts can lead us down a dangerous path. The best we can do is to plan for the future and hope for the best. The reality is that we cannot control our next breath. If we were 100 percent sure of anything in our lives, insurance companies would go out of business. The word for heart used in Hebrew is *leb* and is often associated with our emotions, will, and knowledge. When we follow our own hearts, it means that we are following our own desire for our lives as these parts work together. When it is not aligned with God's will, it will lead us down a path of destruction. When God sits at the center of our hearts, we align ourselves with His desires and ultimately place ourselves on a path of accomplishing the thing we were destined to do. It is our fallen nature that asserts the belief that we don't need God to govern our lives, and many people never discover who they truly are as a result. The modern world asserts self-dependence. Advances in science and technology cause us to falsely believe that we are not in need of salvation, that we are able to live happy, healthy, and completely normal lives on our own. In fact, modern advances in science have created a movement known as transhumanism. This is the blending of man and machine. The enemy can only mimic what God does. Apart from Christ, we cannot have eternal life, yet medical science is seeking to create immortality through human means. It just goes to show how far humanity will go to attempt to preserve itself apart from God.

Humanity tries to govern itself and seek happiness through means of attaining wealth. Though we may be able to amass all of the world's treasures, in the long run, we know there is something still missing. We also know that despite the beliefs of the early Egyptians, you cannot take your earthly treasures with you when you die. That's why you see celebrities that have all of the treasures of the world yet contend with self-hatred, depression, and lack of peace. Many of which have been brought to drug and alcohol abuse and, in extreme cases, attempted and, at times, a successful attempt at suicide. There is this emptiness in our souls that have us longing for answers to tough questions. What we are experiencing is the heavy price that had to be paid for sin. We are experiencing spiritual death and separation from God. We have fallen out of fellowship with the Creator. We have lost ourselves. We don't come to know ourselves until we know God and who we are to Him. The Garden of Eden is described as a place where God once had perfect fellowship and connection with His creation. Scripture says that we are made in the image of God. It is no surprise that God created us for fellowship. This is reflected in the desire that many of us feel to be loved and cared for by someone. Humans are social creatures. It is easy to fall into a deep depression when we isolate ourselves and block out the rest of the world. Every human desires to be loved and accepted. Everyone needs a friend. This shows us that what God ultimately desires from His creation is a relationship, not the emptiness of religion.

## A God of Love, Not Shame

"Then the Lord God called Adam and said to him, 'Where are you?' So he said, 'I heard Your voice in the garden, and I was afraid because I was naked; and I hid myself'" (Genesis 3:9–10, NKJV).

God is not in heaven looking down on the earth, pointing His finger, trying to shame all of us. This is not the God of the Bible. Shame did not enter the picture until a choice was made by Adam and Eve to try to do things their own way according to what they believed was right. Through the act of disobedience in the garden, Adam and Eve, in their immense guilt, tried to hide from God. They sewed together fig leaves to hide the shame of their nakedness. The natural response when we learn about Jesus is that we hide from the immense guilt of sin. We would rather not believe in a God who despises sin because it is in this light that the picture we have painted of ourselves is exposed. Pride prevents us from admitting our shortcomings, and we would rather embrace these behaviors as markers of identity or blame others for our poor choices. The good news is that we don't have to hide from God. He wants to pardon our sins and receive us as sons and daughters. Not only does He want to forgive us of our sins, but He wants to break the chains that hold us down. Sin only produces greater levels of disconnection and pain in our lives. God being a loving teacher, desires to show us how to live in the right relationships with Him, ourselves, and those around us. I spent a lot of my life not really knowing who I was, feeling shame when I made mistakes, and always striving for perfection. I fell into a deep depression and feelings of hopelessness with no real desire to live. This caused me to believe that I was alone and nobody liked me. When I look back on this situation, I recognize that the lenses of pain through which I viewed the world painted a wrong picture about myself, God, and the friends that I did have. I walked

135

through life believing the people who hurt me did so because it was my fault and not because they, too, were imperfect humans in need of a relationship with our Creator.

I was radically delivered from depression, anxiety, and a negative self-image in 2018. I was filled with a love I had never felt before and abundant peace. My life completely changed from there. It was that encounter with God that not only proved His existence but the immense love He had toward me. He took away all of the shame and guilt that I had allowed to creep in as part of my identity. He showed me that I didn't have to hide from Him. Not only did He break those things that had a hold over my life for so many years, but He also gave me a task. He told me to go and tell people what was done for me. Go and tell others of His love and power to break every chain of darkness. Go and tell them that the God of Israel is alive and at work today. Go and tell them that the finished work on the cross made it possible for you to know me. God doesn't want you to hide from Him but to run into His arms.

The world has not known such a powerful love. Sometimes the greatness of God's love can seem even impossible for us to accept. That's why we spend so much time searching for it in other things. We look for it at parties, with friends, at football games, and in clubs. There is only one way to so great a fellowship with the Creator of the world, and His name is Jesus Christ. Keep in mind the world may try to offer solutions to your emptiness, depression, loneliness, frustration, and anxieties. The world's solutions may work for a time, but they will ultimately fail. There is only one thing that cannot fail, and that is a loving and perfect God. All of your prior methods of searching for fulfillment will bottom out at some point. This can be when a relationship ends or when the partying impacts your grades. It could be when you lose a job, or you're overlooked for an award. These methods of escaping shame only ever bring temporary relief. I like to think of the solutions the world gives us as a pill to our problems. You can take a pill for a headache, but did the headache really go away? You may not be able to feel the headache, but the medicine only numbed you to the problem. The same thing goes for our souls. Did the wound really go away, or have we numbed ourselves so that we can no longer feel it? Thankfully, Jesus Christ came to bring healing to our souls by the transforming power of the Father's love.

**The Result of Sin in the World**

"So when the woman saw that the tree was good for food, that it was pleasant to the eyes, and a tree desirable to make one wise, she took of its fruit and ate" (Genesis 3:6, NKJV).

We can take one look at the world and see that the biblical account of the fall of mankind answers every question concerning the evil we encounter. A consequence of sin is the world that we see around us. There is poverty, disease, violence, and injustice. As humans, we tend to react pridefully and say things like, "I'm a good person." When in reality, if this were universally true (humans are innately good), then we wouldn't live in the world that we do. All of the issues in society are a result of human choice. Mankind follows after its own will in an attempt to please the self. This is the core teaching of many

Eastern philosophies, such as Buddhism, which is about relieving oneself from suffering. There is no offer of selfless love to bring peace to a dying world, which is what Christ taught His disciples. Let me give you an example of this truth in the average American home. Ask yourself this question honestly. Would you be willing to give up your gaming device, your second car, or that yearly vacation in order to feed others? How about to get them clean water? Most people would not, and this is because we are innately prideful and self-seeking. It's a hard pill to swallow when we realize that our intentions are not as pure as we want to convince ourselves. This is not to say that humans can't or don't do any good in the world. However, it is not our natural disposition when push comes to shove. We want to walk in a way that is pleasing to ourselves. We may give a dollar or two to the beggar in the street or open the door for someone walking into the store. If we evaluate the intent behind this work, it is typically one of self, where we feel good about what we have done. It becomes less about doing something nice for the other person and more about feeling proud that we have done something good. Is the work done really about helping others or about relieving yourself of the guilt you may feel for not doing the right thing?

God often gets the blame for much of the world's evil. I know that I was angry at God, questioning why He would let all of these terrible things happen. Yet, I wanted to be an agent of free will, given the ability to choose my own course of happiness. God could wipe out the entire Earth if He chooses to do so, but instead, He allows us the ability to make a choice. Unfortunately, due to our disobedient and self-seeking nature, our choices are the very reason there is so much suffering in the world. If we want to understand the condition of the world, we must address the inner wounds that bring pain to ourselves and those around us. Despite humanity's best efforts to make the world a better place, someone will always lose out. This is the result of a world governed by human reasoning and not by the infinite wisdom of the Creator. People have decided to live according to what is right in their own minds and not through moral absolutes. We say we want absolute equality but not at the expense of our own self-satisfaction. I'll ask the question again. What are you going to sell so someone else can be clothed or fed? You probably wouldn't sell anything, and if you did, it would be to avoid looking like a bad person. If you want more proof as to how this imbalance in our world is evident, just look at celebrities. So many celebrities live in excess, while others don't even have a roof over their head. Many of which are pro-communistic ideologies. Which house are you going to give up to make that a reality? Which car are you willing to sell? The most common rebuttal I hear to the points made above is, "Well, why doesn't God do something about it?" We blame God because we know that He can change any situation. He will not just simply end all evil until all of the biblical prophecies written come to pass and a new chapter in the earth begins. There will be a true utopia when Jesus comes to reign as King on Earth after all of the biblical prophecies come to pass. The Bible does speak consistently about the fact that justice for harming the innocent will come. There will be a day where each person will give an account of how they lived their lives on Earth. We have a choice in how we live our lives, and we were not created to be slaves. Something God laid on my heart early in our relationship was that, had humanity not fallen, we would have never known evil. If we didn't know evil, we couldn't be drawn away from Him and His abundant love. God's love is so immense for His creation that He goes to the utmost extremes to restore what was lost in the garden.

## Two Trees, Two Paths

> And out of the ground the Lord God made every tree grow that is pleasant to the sight and good for food. The tree of life was also in the midst of the garden, and the tree of the knowledge of good and evil.
>
> Genesis 2:9 (NKJV)

The Bible has many parables concerning seeds, trees, and fruit. I would like to draw your attention to the fact that there were two trees present in the Genesis account. So many people only focus on the tree of the knowledge of good and evil. There was also a tree that gave eternal life. If we look at our own spiritual condition, we learn that we fall into one of two categories. We either abide in Christ or in the world. We are either governed by God or by the world. Our knowledge is either life (coming from the tree of life) or death (coming from the tree of knowledge of good and evil). Just as two trees were placed in the garden allowing Adam and Eve a choice to live in fellowship with God, we too have a choice.

The tree of the knowledge of good and evil is one that leads to spiritual death.[32] We are born into this category. We have disobedient hearts, naturally yearning to fulfill the lusts and desires of the flesh. The flesh loves sin. The roots of this tree are firmly planted in pride. To reiterate, pride is saying, "I can do it, and I don't need a Savior." The moment the seed of rebellion was planted into our hearts, we began to bear the fruit of that tree.[33] The result is spiritual death. A key point to keep in mind here is that God made every tree to grow that was pleasant to the sight and good for food. This tree, according to Eve, had another feature. It was also a tree desirable to make one wise.[34] Human desire, lust, and the will of mankind to govern itself are all spiritual implications of the fruit this tree has to offer. This tree did not look harmful. The fruit, in fact, probably looked great. Sin is kind of like that. It doesn't seem so bad; in fact, it may be fun for a season, but it ultimately does not lead to anything good. We fall into sin through the same means by which Eve was tempted in the Garden of Eden. A powerful lesson on temptation can be found in 1 John 2:16 (NKJV), which reads, "For all that is in the world—the lust of the flesh, the lust of the eyes, and the pride of life—is not of the Father but is of the world."

Let's break this down further.

**The Lust of the Eyes**

"So when the woman saw that the tree was good for food, *that it was pleasant to the eyes*, and a tree desirable to make one wise, she took of its fruit and ate" (Genesis 3:6, NKJV) (emphasis by the author).

When Eve saw the forbidden tree, it was pleasant to the eye. Sin is viewed as something that looks good on the outside but brings death and corruption once you indulge. One major tactic used by the enemy today is our phones. We are exposed to so much on social media platforms, and you have the entire world right in your pocket. We see people going on vacations, posting their best selfies, and boasting about their accomplishments. It isn't hard to start feeling jealousy or becoming obsessed with the lives of seemingly successful people. We see the promise of wealth in fast cars, expensive clothes, and access to the right people for career success. So many people are lured into the ways of the world through the promise of wealth and celebrity status. In the long run, it is all empty. You don't know the thoughts of celebrities when they lay down at night. None of that life brings true fulfillment. They still feel alone, though surrounded by a multitude of people. They don't show you the truth behind the camera. You only see what they want you to see. Isn't it the same way for you? When you post something online, you're usually highlighting your best self. The cyber-world is not reality. Yet we mold our lives to fit this image of what appears to be success, leading to the superficial happiness that the world claims to offer. That does not mean you cannot be a Christian who is successful or well-known. It just means that your joy and fulfillment are not defined through material possessions.

## The Lust of the Flesh

"*So when the woman saw that the tree was good for food*, that it was pleasant to the eyes, and a tree desirable to make one wise, she took of its fruit and ate" (Genesis 3:6, NKJV) (emphasis by the author).

The lust of the flesh would be things that seem like a great idea at the moment. These are things that make us feel good temporarily. Things we think we need, like a wild night in the city getting drunk with friends. There are repercussions for these actions. You end up spending the next day hungover, confused, and disoriented. You have no idea what you did the night before and lost your wallet or your keys. Maybe you got into a fight and were thrown out of the party or landed yourself a night in prison. There are consequences for actions, and the flesh response is usually to blame others for our own poor choices. Another example we often see when working with married couples is infidelity. Your flesh may say at the moment that it is okay to cheat because you deserve to be happy. Sure, it may feel great for that moment. You may think, *I am unhappy in my relationship and this person will give me something that I need.* In the long run, you are going to feel guilty, and it will somehow be exposed. God brings to light all things done in darkness.[35] Your dirty laundry will be aired sooner or later. Hearts will be broken, and relationships will be ruined. If the relationship continues, there will be mistrust at the very least, and a path to restoration would be needed to reconcile the damage. The lust of the flesh connects with the works of the flesh and is not limited to the examples provided here.

**The Pride of Life**

"So when the woman saw that the tree was good for food, that it was pleasant to the eyes, *and a tree desirable to make one wise*, she took of its fruit and ate" (Genesis 3:6, NKJV) (emphasis by the author).

This has two applications, and they are pride and lust. Pride says we don't need God. We are proud of who we are, and there is no need for us to change. Scripture says that God gives grace to the humble but resists the proud. Pride stands in the way of us knowing Christ and seeing change in the world. Modern American culture views pride as a good thing. We have nationalistic pride, gay pride, cultural pride, sports pride, regional pride, and other things that make us proud. From a Christian perspective, pride is the very thing that leads to our destruction. Have you ever met somebody that refused to change? No matter how nicely you talk to them or how much love you show them, they still refuse to admit their faults. That's pride. It is something that needs to be broken in us in order for us to truly grow. Desire is lusting after things in this world. The disciples of Christ were told to sell their possessions and follow Him. Christ is the utmost example of humility. The strongest desire had become about doing the Father's will. I am not telling you to go and sell all of your stuff. However, if you want to grow in the kingdom of God, your desire for things offered by the world must decrease. This will free you to follow Christ and become obedient to the will of God. When we have fewer attachments to the things of this world, we are able to give of ourselves to God in greater measure. This does not mean that you cannot desire things. When our hearts are aligned with God's will, He gives us the desires of our hearts because His desires become our desires.

## The Tree of Life

The seed for this tree is planted when one hears the message of the gospel. When one hears this message, the condition of the soil (the heart) determines the fate of the seed. This is demonstrated through the parable of the sower, which is found in Matthew 13. If planted in good soil, it eventually grows into a tree. This tree is rooted in Christ, who was an example of humility. Being rooted in Christ brings eternal life. The fruit we then bear, through the life-giving sap of the Holy Spirit in every believer, is then good.[36] This tree also brings healing to the nations, as expressed in the book of Revelation. We can see that it is only through abiding in Christ and the governing of God that the nations themselves will see freedom from violence, poverty, illness, and other forms of destruction.

What we see taking place in the natural world is a good indication of what is happening spiritually. A person who is firmly rooted in Christ will benefit from the healing of their soul. Let me ask you a question. If we were all planted firmly in Christ, submitted to the will of God, and governed by the Holy Spirit, wouldn't the world look quite different? Christ uses the parable of "The Vine and the Branches" found in John 15:1–17 to explain that without Him, we can do nothing. We are not able to bear this good fruit through human effort. The core foundation of all other belief systems requires working your way to freedom or salvation. This is impossible to do. That is a way of relying on your human effort to save you from the consequences of sin. Without Christ, we are but a cursed tree, withering away. Any effort we muster up to be good is futile in the weakness of our humanity. Human goodness is temporary, fleeting, empty, and dead. Fortunately, through Christ, we can bear good fruit. An important takeaway from the Garden of Eden account is that the disobedience of one couple brought spiritual death and condemnation to humanity. In order to justify this grievous error on behalf of the human race, Jesus Christ took the full punishment of sin on the cross to bring salvation to humanity. The price to pay for our sin was death.

## Called to Share the Gospel

"You are My witnesses," says the Lord, "And My servant whom I have chosen, That you may know and believe Me, And understand that I am He. Before Me there was no God formed, Nor shall there be after Me."

Isaiah 43:10 (NKJV)

Age and number of years in school do not matter when it comes to the gospel. We are all called to share the good news of salvation. The word salvation is often tossed around in Christianity. What does this mean? What is the gospel? What is the new covenant? The terms gospel and covenant are important for understanding salvation. We spoke about how sin leads to spiritual death and separation from God. Here comes the scary truth. Remember how we said that God is one of justice? There has to be a punishment for sin. Scripture describes that after the final judgment, the eternal resting place for the wicked would be in the lake of fire.[37] If you want to call it a resting place at all because not much resting will be taking place. You might be thinking, *Well, that seems a bit harsh.* I used to feel that way. What I didn't understand is that God is eternal, and because we are offered eternal life, the punishment for sin must also be eternal. This punishment is actually the utmost form of justice, and that desire to see justice served is within humanity. You may be thinking, *Isn't God love? Why punish this way?* The truth is that hell was never meant for you. It was because of mankind's disobedience in the garden that

147

our hearts turned away from God's love and turned to ourselves and doing things that lead to sin. Hell was created for the fallen angels who rebelled against God. Satan knows he is condemned, and because you are made in God's image, he wants to take as many of God's precious creations with him into a godless eternity. We must retrain our thoughts around this issue. God does not send people to hell. That is our natural disposition. We are all heading there and unable to save ourselves. When we understand things from this perspective, God's mercy is on full display, and He no longer seems like this savage tyrant hell-bent on destroying humanity. There is one who fits that description, and it's not your creator.

The gospel means good news. What exactly is this good news? You don't have to live out eternity in anguish. Salvation has been made available through the sacrifice of Jesus Christ on the cross. Jesus was sent in order to reconcile humanity back to the Father. Through the payment of the debt that we owed, we are able to come back into a close fellowship with God. A sort of inner restoration of the intimacy once shared in the garden. Our flesh nature desires to sin, and when ruled by this nature, we are enemies in our hearts and minds toward God. This is why we are commanded to love our enemies. In doing so, we take on the nature of Christ, where God loved us while we were His enemies. The Bible tells us, "But God demonstrates His own love toward us, in that while we were yet sinners, Christ died for us" (Romans 5:8, NASB). Our sin made us like criminals who have all broken God's perfect law. God's law shows us where we fall short of the standard set for heavenly perfection. Each and every one of us has a criminal record in the kingdom of heaven because we have all broken at least one if not many of God's laws. We will all stand before God one day and have to give an account for our lives.[38] Those who have accepted the sacrifice of Jesus Christ as their personal Savior have had their record of sin wiped clean. The debt or punishment that would have been ours was paid in full by Jesus Christ through the sacrifice of His life. Imagine you were on trial for a crime you committed. You were found guilty and merely waiting for sentencing. You receive the death penalty. When in comes an innocent man who committed no crime but offers to take the sentence for you. Would you take it? This is what Jesus did. He served a sentence for you. He took on physical death so that God could give you eternal life. Those who do not accept the Son are still enemies of God. They continue on in a lifestyle of sin, not knowing the Father. Those who repent (change their mind) about sin and put their faith in Jesus Christ by surrendering their lives to Him are born again. We are given a new nature. The first gift we then receive as a new creation in Christ is the Holy Spirit. The Holy Spirit enables us to live the Christian lifestyle having victory over the flesh and sin in our lives. It is important to understand these concepts not only to ensure our own salvation but to witness to others the free gift offered by God. We must all become a new creation.

The new nature is a heart that is turned toward wanting to do the will of God and not toward wanting to do our own will to follow after the flesh. This is part of the new covenant. God promises to write His laws on our hearts and minds,[39] enabling us to follow Him. We are no longer enemies but sons and daughters. He changes our hearts by changing our thoughts, wants, and desires to be aligned with His will. God's standards are high, and He came to show us the problem was in our hearts. I don't mean your heart as in the place that pumps blood through your body. The heart is more of the control center that regulates our intellect, emotions, and will. This means that we need to focus on our thoughts and desires, which eventually lead to action. The standard God sets for us is high because He is not looking only at our actions but our hearts, where the ideas for actions originate.[40] The more we allow God to be at the center of our hearts, the more we become like Him and less likely to act out in a sinful manner. Many will agree that cheating on your husband or wife is wrong. Jesus declares this truth in Matthew 5:28 (NKJV), "But I say to you that whoever looks at a woman to lust for her has already committed adultery with her in his heart." This shows that before a physical action ever occurred, a sickness of the heart was present. It seems nearly impossible to change your thoughts, but with God, all things are possible. There are plenty of self-help books that tell you how to change your thinking, but without God, we cannot overcome the flesh nature.[41] We need supernatural heart surgery. When you choose to give your life to Christ, you are given a fresh start and a new purpose, and you will begin on a journey to become more like Jesus each day. The new covenant (promise) was sealed by the blood of Christ. This was an eternal sacrifice that we can express gratitude for at the highest level because what was done for us on the cross will cover all of our shortcomings. We then have Jesus Christ as an advocate for us. When you pray, He hears and acts on our behalf for our good. This is the beauty of salvation. He gave us spiritual life, circumcised our hearts (enabling us to want to do God's will), and wrote His laws on our hearts and minds. When we obey the will of the flesh, the result is separation from God and spiritual death. Until Jesus gives us new life in Him, we are slaves to this fallen nature and will continue in cycles of defeat. God is calling us to place our trust in Him to lead us. He becomes the shepherd of our souls. He is a good shepherd too.[42] He will lead you on the right path and lovingly draw you back should you wander away from Him. Walking with God does not mean you need to be perfect. It just means you have a heart after His own heart, and you grow a little more each day.

A lot of people you will speak to have little to no idea of the true gospel. They may have heard a works-based gospel or some other gospel that is not good news at all. This does not mean that people don't have an idea of what the gospel could be based on previously made judgments. This may mean some are instantly closed off to the mere idea of having a conversation about Jesus. As you grow in your relationship with the Lord, you will be more tuned to His voice and leading. There were times in some classes when the Lord called me to be still and observe. Other times, He would highlight a specific student, and this was who I was called to tell about Him. One specific instance I can recall was during the first year of my master's program. Another student was outside of the school with that same group I mentioned earlier who were protesting against law enforcement at the height of the BLM movement. I spoke with him briefly and expressed a Christian viewpoint on the matter, being one of living in mutual understanding and extending a hand of peace. We discussed God's prevailing justice over matters and that to see any change in our world, we must be able to converse peaceably with one another. He listened to my words, and I could see something change inside. He later told me that His mother was a born-again believer and he had wandered away from those teachings but that my words resonated deeply with him. He told me that he had a lot to think about. God is good like that. He will show you whose heart is ready, and we must be willing to answer the call to plant the seed if the opportunity arises. This is far different than the approach of some street preachers who speak mostly about condemnation. I have nothing against street preaching; in fact, I think it's one of the hardest things to do. You face a lot of rejection and really need to walk in love. However, I think it's wise to know your crowd and to have an appropriate approach to successfully reach people for Christ. A lot of people don't want to be preached but are looking to be understood. We can seek to understand those around us without necessarily agreeing with what they do.

Perhaps one of the more difficult circumstances you may face is those who outright reject hearing anything about Jesus. This is where your walk is so important. I once had a co-worker who expressed that she admired the way I handled a particularly difficult circumstance. I thanked her for the praise but let her know that it wasn't done in my own strength. This opened another fruitful conversation. I later learned that she, too, grew up in a Christian household but walked away from the faith after experiencing some church hurt. I was able to discuss a similar experience, and I know God worked through me to plant a seed in a woman He so dearly loved. We may not know why people reject the gospel, but we can ask for insight from the Holy Spirit and be good listeners. This will allow us to not only be those who hear God's Word but those who do God's Word. Our actions and our words are an effective way to lead others to the Lord. Some people do not recognize their need for salvation. They are self-assured, self-reliant, self-confident, and think they have it all figured out. That's usually the case until something tragic happens, or you find yourself in a circumstance that no human means can truly solve. This is where God can work in an even greater way.

The first time I went out in the streets to try to speak to people for the Lord, I have to admit, was nerve-wracking. God was faithful, and He drew me to speak to a man who had been sitting in the park. I later learned that he was recently released from prison for a previous conviction of murder. He said that some evangelists came and told him his sin was too much and he couldn't be saved. I told him about Paul and what he had done and how God not only saved him but accomplished so much through him. His heart was so ready to receive the Lord, and we prayed together. He accepted the Lord into his life, and I gave him a Bible. Not everyone understands what he did about life. Many of us take life for granted. He understood that tomorrow was not promised. Anything can happen. We cannot stop ourselves from tragic things that can happen in life. We have very little control over many aspects of our life. The number one excuse I hear from young people is that they want to live their lives now and maybe do the church stuff later. They don't want to miss out on all the fun. What they don't realize is just how precious our lives are and that there is no guarantee that we will see morning. Do you really want to go through your life that way? How much more beautiful can life be if you have someone caring for your every need? The God of all creation invites you to know Him on a personal level. You will come to know that you will be loved, and He will provide for your needs. In Hebrew, one of the names of God given by Abraham is Jehovah-Jireh. This means God provides. Other Old Testament names for God are Jehovah-Nissi (The Lord my banner), Jehovah-Raah (The Lord my shepherd), Jehovah-Rapha (The Lord that heals), Jehovah-Shammah (The Lord is there), Jehovah-Tsidkenu (The Lord our righteousness), Jehovah-Mekoddishkem (The Lord who sanctifies you), Jehovah-Shalom (The Lord is peace), Jehovah-Sabbath (The Lord of hosts). God can literally do anything, and He delights in caring for us.

If you do not know Jesus Christ as your personal Savior, or you want to know how to lead others into a relationship with God, I would invite you to pray and ask Him to be your Savior. Make the decision to turn away from living a lifestyle of sin and place your trust in God to lead you. Surrender your life to Jesus. If you do know Him as your Savior, then this section is important in leading others to Christ. How exactly does one come to salvation? How do you enter into a promised relationship and adoption as a son or daughter of the Most High? Although different denominations will say different things, here is what you really need to know. We leave the rest up to God to do His work. This is a free gift for anyone who believes and puts their faith in

Jesus Christ.[43] First, you must believe. Acts 16:31 (NKJV), "So they said, 'Believe on the Lord Jesus Christ, and you will be saved, you and your household.'" Scripture talks a lot about belief. We must believe in Jesus and what He did for us. Belief is tied to faith. We show that we believe by placing our trust in God. We must also believe that He died and rose again, conquering death, hell, and sin.

The next thing the Bible tells us is to repent. Luke 24:46–47 (NKJV),

> Then He said to them, "Thus it is written, and thus it was necessary for the Christ to suffer and to rise from the dead the third day, and that repentance and remission of sins should be preached in His name to all nations, beginning at Jerusalem."

A largely debated topic today is if repentance is necessary for salvation. Repentance is key! Repentance is making the decision (given by free will) to turn away from your sin. You are bringing yourself into an agreement with God about sin. Turning away from sin is a willful act of obedience toward God. We are told we need to confess. Romans 10:9–10 (NKJV),

> If you confess with your mouth the Lord Jesus and believe in your heart that God has raised Him from the dead, you will be saved. For with the heart one believes unto righteousness, and with the mouth confession is made unto salvation.

Confession is necessary. This is different than going to a priest and confessing your sins, as taught in the Catholic church. Here you are making a confession of faith before an Almighty God. When we make this confession of faith, we are declaring that we believe the truth and intend to begin our lives as Christians. Confession of sins tends to also occur. When God begins to change your heart, things that you have done wrong tend to come out as we seek God for forgiveness. As we confess these things, we are stating in our own words that we do not want these things to be a part of us. What follows shortly after is baptism. There is both a physical baptism and a baptism of the Holy Spirit. John 3:5 (NKJV) states, "Jesus answered, 'Most assuredly, I say to you, unless one is born of water and the Spirit, he cannot enter the kingdom of God.'" Water baptism is an outward expression of what is taking place in the spiritual. We are being washed clean and made new. Another symbolic application is that it is a funeral. You are entering the water and partaking in Christ's death, showing the death of the old self (sinful lifestyle) and the birth (in Spirit) and resurrection into the body of Christ and new life. It is a chance to have witnesses present to see that you have chosen to live your life for Jesus. Perhaps one of the most important things when becoming a believer in Jesus Christ is to remain faithful. We must persevere in the faith. Remember, it is faith in Jesus Christ that saves us. We are being delivered from new things every single day. You may go through some rough times, but do not leave the one who loves you most. Your faith will be tested and tried so that God can mature you. You may experience difficult seasons, but you can trust that He will continue the work that He started. I think it's very important to connect with a Spirit-filled church. It is so important to have fellowship. This does not mean your church will be perfect but never let that remove the faith you've placed in Jesus. We shouldn't give people that much power over us and our relationship with Him. Invest in a nice Bible. I personally love a good study Bible because there is historical context in some of the footnotes, which brings the Word to life in an amazing way. The Word of God will become a source of life to you. It will combat every lie that may come into your mind, and God uses it to speak to us. It will sanctify you and teach you to walk in the ways of God. The Bible will become your daily bread (spiritual food) which is essential for your growth in the faith. Ask God to bring other believers into your life that can help you along the way. He gave us each other to help and encourage one another in this walk. Above all, nurture your relationship with God, and it will grow beautifully, and you will too.

## Do You Really Know Yourself?

But as many as received Him, to them He gave the right to become children of God, to those who believe in His name.

John 1:12 (NKJV)

One of the most powerful and liberating things is to come into the revelation of your identity in Christ. The world around us is constantly offering answers to tell us who we are. If you have given your life to Christ and are living for Him, then we understand who we are by connecting with whose we are. The world teaches us that identity is rooted in things and images. Where you were born, who you love, and what you like are all markers of identity. The problem here is that we can be easily influenced in these areas. Add on the mindset of compartmentalization, and now you believe you know who you are, and you search for others who are like you. You feel temporary happiness and a desire to defend your ever-evolving identity through the protection mechanisms that were learned over time. You may believe that because you feel something, it must mean that it's true and it's who you are. These mindsets are harmful and never address the nagging empty feeling inside. It never truly gets to the root of why there is a need to fight so hard for who you think you are. When someone is truly confident that they know themselves, there is no need to defend or fight. If we establish our identity in Christ, we are sure to move forward in life on the strongest foundation possible. An identity in Christ establishes our worth and our purpose. There have been a number of days when I didn't feel like I was a child of God, but that doesn't mean it isn't who I am. In fact, I believe it takes a lifetime of seeking and intimacy with God to ever truly know the fullness of who we are. What makes you who you are? What are the metrics you use to define yourself? Is that something that is serving you well, or do you feel the need to constantly defend your identity?

I didn't always believe I was a child of God. In fact, my teenage and college years were characterized by trying to figure out where I fit. I thought that if my hair was a certain way, or if I liked a type of music, then I could find where I fit in. The problem was I never felt like I truly fit anywhere. Humans like to box things up into neat packages with defined borders. God did not design us to fit one cookie-cutter mold but created us all unique with a specific purpose to fulfill. Each box that I tried to place myself in came with certain stigmatizations that I also needed to defend because it's who I am, right? If you had asked me who I was at that time, I would have told you, "My name is Daniella Marie, and I grew up in Brooklyn, New York. My family is pretty traditionally Italian, and yes, we eat pasta at 2 p.m. on Sundays. I am an honor roll student and an actress. I am a writer and a waitress part-time." That's what I would have said to you. I had a lot of "I am" statements. There was no separation between who I was and what I did. This is probably one of the biggest differences between life as a believer in Jesus and the thinking pattern of the world. If you were to ask me this question today, I would say something far shorter than this. I would say that I am a daughter of God. All of my old markers of identity are not who I am, but they are what I do or what I like. All of the other things can be taken away from me. When our identity is founded on what we do or what we have, we are sure to feel a deep sense of lack when that thing is taken away from us, or we experience a difficult life change. This is why it is so devastating for some who lose their jobs or fail in school. There is identity attached to it. We can fail in performing and living up to the label attached to our name. We then begin to believe that we have no place in the world and our life is without meaning. This can lead to deep depression and even suicide. I was there. I felt that. My deepest fear was failure. Failure meant I had no place or purpose. This is called the orphan spirit. We were not called to be orphans, wandering through the earth searching for meaning and position. We are called to be sons and daughters of God. We must understand our position in Christ as children, not in the way our physical parents displayed love and authority (be it positive or negative), but in the way that a perfect Father knows. We step into a new level of understanding ourselves, our purpose, and the direction in which we have been called to walk.

There are some essential understandings that we must adopt in order to know more deeply who we are. Firstly, know that you have been created in God's image. Genesis 1:27 (NKJV) states, "So God created man in His own image; in the image of God He created him; male and female He created them." I find it fascinating how people who do not yet know God are often bothered by the very things He shares in common with His creation. We judge God for getting angry and protecting His people, yet we share that very same quality. God understands us more than we understand ourselves and shares qualities with us. God gets angry, but don't you? God gets sad, but don't you? God loves deeply, but don't you? God desires justice, but don't you? As I stated before, you are made in His image. The biggest difference is that God's anger, sadness, love, and justice are on a much greater scale than ours. God doesn't make mistakes, and so His anger, sadness, love, and desire for justice are perfect and come from a perfectly pure place. Ours doesn't always.

God created you to be special and for fellowship with Him. Much of what the world offers as reasoning for your creation is a mere accident. The theory of evolution provides that you are here by random chance and that we happened to evolve from monkeys. I may not be a scientist or the most qualified person to provide an in-depth response as to why macroevolution is not real science, apart from some logical fallacies in the arguments that I can see. I can, however, provide you with a very real understanding of the emotional toll carrying such a belief has on the human psyche. If we take on the belief that our existence is a mere accident and that we are nothing more than a little speck in some vast universe, then what's the point? The Bible teaches that each individual life is precious and set apart for a purpose. Not everyone is able to obtain the fullness of the truth of their God-given purpose because there is a very real battle for each soul. However, each individual life is formed by God and is ultimately precious. He even knows how many hairs are on your head.[44] This is a God of careful calculations and great attention to detail. Are you starting to feel a little less like an accident of cosmic soup?

To fully mold your identity, you need to know that you are not merely an accident and that Darwinian evolution cannot be proven on the macro-level. It continues to remain a theory and science's best theory. The issue is that you cannot truly ever document millions of years of the evolution of one species to become another species. True science is measurable from the inception of the idea through the process of testing, which should lead to some sort of conclusion. I am pretty sure that millions of years ago, there were no scientists around. Even in the last 2 thousand years, scientists have only been able to give their best guesses which have changed many times and are sure to change again. I actually believe true science observes what is present and true science reveals the truth of God as Creator. It seeks to understand more deeply what is available to be studied or explored. The problem comes when the idea of observation is transferred to theoretical science. You can observe and hypothesize, but nothing can be deemed as a fact or a law without sufficient evidence. No mammal in history has ever been observed to transform from one animal into another completely, and this is macroevolution. Microevolution does exist, where there are different variations within each kind of animal. This is actually what Darwin observed when on the Galapagos Islands. He observed several variations of bird species and theorized they must have evolved over time and adapted to their environment. His observation only proved that birds remained birds with some changes. It did not observe that a fish eventually became a human. In a spiritual sense, the idea of transforming from one thing to another has a parallel in Christian and Gnostic teaching. For a Christian, a human is transformed from the Adamic flesh nature to a new creation in Christ.

When a person receives Jesus as their Savior, they become in-dwelt with the Holy Spirit. There is a real noticeable change in attitudes, desires, and lifestyle choices. Many early and well-known scientists were also Gnostics who dabbled in the mystery religions. Gnostics also believe in a type of transformation. However, there is a belief that one can evolve into a state of godhood. This goes back to the lie told by the serpent in the garden—that when eating the fruit of the knowledge of good and evil, their eyes would be opened, and they would be like God. I believe the secular teaching of macroevolution is framed in such a way to make the Gnostic teaching of soul transformation into godhood not only more palatable but widely accepted and celebrated. *The Apotheosis of Washington*, a mural painted on the eye of the U. S. Capitol Building's rotunda, depicts this Gnostic teaching of the first American president ascending into godhood. Isn't it interesting that the eyes are what the serpent promised would open so humans could be gods, and here we see a supposed ascent to godhood painted on the eye of the U. S. Capitol Building?

There has always been a desire in the heart of God to be close to His creation. In creating you to reflect His image, you became a target to our common enemy, previously known as Lucifer, the fallen angel. If Satan (Lucifer) can draw you away from God, tempt you to sin against God, and ultimately grieve God's heart, then his mission has been accomplished. The enemy never wants you to come into the truth of who you are by coming into a relationship with the one who made you. The truth is that it is less about you and more about the enemy's attempt to hurt God by hurting you. What is most important to understand here is that you are extremely valuable and must recognize that a war has been waged in the spirit, which manifests itself in our physical world, for the destruction or salvation of your soul. Satan is condemned, and there is no chance for him or demons who are fallen with him to be redeemed. There is a chance for you.

We are bought with the ultimate sacrifice of Jesus Christ, shedding His blood for us on the cross. This was done to redeem us back to the Father so that we may have fellowship once again with God. We need to start identifying ourselves as wanted by God and extremely valuable. Jesus explains just how important you are, and I would beg to say that if you are reading this right now, God is calling you to know Him. John 6:44 (NKJV) explains, "No one can come to Me unless the Father who sent Me draws him; and I will raise him up at the last day." Please understand that the Father does not want to see any of His creations destroyed. Those who are in Christ have had the price for our sin paid through the sacrifice of Jesus. Place your identity in Christ, and read what the Bible says about the promises available to God's children. This is a key piece to Christian spiritual growth. When we read the Bible, it is meant to be a big mirror. The Bible really reads us. Who does God say that you are? Does it align with who you think you are? Anything founded outside of what the Bible says about who you are is sure to fail, and our hope cannot be placed there. To take it a step further, consider whether or not these scriptures feel true to you. If they don't feel true, ask God to show you why because His Word is truth, and this is truly who you are in Him if you know Him.

## Do You Really Know God?

God is not a man, that He should lie, Nor a son of man,
that He should repent. Has He said, and will He not do?
Or has He spoken, and will He not make it good?

Numbers 23:19 (NKJV)

I believe that God is one of the most misunderstood beings in
existence. When we don't know the truth about God, the education
system can paint any picture they'd like about Him. There are well over
a hundred different ways in which God is referred to in the Bible. All
of which are meant to reveal something about His character. Some
of these names are El Elyon (God Most High), El Roi (God who
sees), El Shaddai (All-sufficient God), Jehovah-Jireh (Jehovah will
provide), Jehovah-Rapha (Jehovah who heals), Jehovah-Nissi (God
my banner), Jehovah-Mekoddishkem (God who sanctifies you),
Jehovah-Shalom (God is peace), Jehovah-Raah (God my shepherd),
Jehovah-Tsidkenu (God our saving justice), and so much more. The
Bible pretty clearly outlines the characteristics of God, so why do we
turn Him into a version with which we feel most comfortable? All of
the names used to refer to God are good, so we can trust that He is
a good God and that His Word sets the standard for what is good. I
used to always say, "I believe in a higher being, but not God, like in
the Bible." Why do we do this? Well, it makes us more comfortable.
You see, we want to live in a way that allows us to do whatever we
want without being accountable for the consequences that come

along with how we choose to live. I strongly believe that most of the world has some opinion concerning God's character. Particularly that of the Christian God. If you go to a more extreme view, some even deny God's existence because they cannot understand God or why He would allow so much suffering. Instead, it is easier to reject the notion of a God that does not fit in with what I want to believe. I hear people say, "I think God is (fill in the blank)." They have an opinion about God that goes against the revelation of the Word of God as it was revealed in the Bible. This does not define God; it only creates an idol.

I believe that this is what God was referring to when He told us not to make idols. False gods often have human attributes that are unique to the god. However, false gods are made in the image of man; when man was truly made in the image of God. When humans cannot create a false image of God, they move to claim that He does not exist. It is this mind of skepticism that looks to the Bible and sees an inconsistent God full of contradictions. So the logical conclusion is to deny His existence entirely? To the skeptical mind, the Bible is irrational: virgin births, slaying giants, talking serpents, and raising from the dead. This is why the Bible tells us that we cannot discern spiritual things through human reasoning or a mind that is not being renewed. It is the Holy Spirit that gives us insight, wisdom, and revelation considering the Word of God. Apart from the guidance of the Holy Spirit, none would understand the heavenly truths shared with us. As a result of the lack of understanding, some people have based their beliefs on a twisted view of Scripture. We create a God we are okay with serving based on our own personal experiences, failed faith, judgments toward God, criticisms toward the church, and poor examples of Christian leadership. We judge Him based on the faults of others. What if we judged our friends that way? Instead of trying to get to know our friends, we judge them based on other people's opinions or actions. The same applies to God. What do you believe about God? How did those beliefs get there in the first place? Asking these questions is key to finding long-term breakthroughs in our thinking. We often project the failures of our parents onto God when we think of Him as Father. We project our mother wounds onto the Helper or the Holy Spirit. Sadly, we can even project our friend or sibling wounds onto Jesus. Each aspect of the Godhead signifies very real relationships we see reflected here on Earth. The difference is that God is perfect, and so we must surrender the pain we carry inside that can so easily be projected onto our view of who God is in our lives. Some practical ways to dig deeper into what we believe about God that may be tainting our view of Him are to answer some of the following questions. Who is God to you? What do you believe God thinks about you? When did you first believe that? This self-reflection exercise really shows us a lot about the preconceived ideas we carry about God.

The world often has its own interpretation of the Bible, and I have noticed it takes pieces of Scripture and creates a God that is not consistent with the way He is revealed through the Bible. All throughout Scripture, God is constantly trying to show mankind His heart and His character. The good news is that His Word says that if we ask, He will show us things we do not know.[45] This includes more and more about Himself so that we can know Him on a more intimate level. When I received the baptism of the Holy Spirit, God revealed Himself to me. I had a sort of Paul on the road to Damascus experience. Jesus revealed Himself to Paul, and that day in my car, Jesus revealed Himself to me. I knew it was Jesus and not some other false god because my heart was turned toward the Word of God. This was during a time when I had basically renounced any ties to the Christian faith and was deep into Jain's philosophy and teaching. Something was different that day. I had felt joy and inner peace that I had never experienced. There was an inner knowing that affirmed the words I read in Galatians 5:22.

God invites each of us to seek Him in this way. To ask questions and search His Word for answers. This concept is contrary to the false belief that many hold concerning Christianity, which tells you not to ask questions. Asking questions is a natural part of humanity. It is a part of human development. We don't have to teach children to ask why about practically everything. It is ingrained in our nature. In fact, it is one of the greatest things that separates us from the rest of God's creation. No matter how many monkeys are trained to paint or write out words, not one has ever asked a question. Asking questions is what draws us closer to God if we allow it. Humans have just been asking the wrong question. Instead of asking if God exists, we should be asking about who God is. I believe there are three core aspects of His nature that we must acknowledge in order to have a fuller picture of God. The three aspects of God that are most important to grasp are God the Father, God our Healer, and God the Judge.

## God the Father

"Do not call anyone on earth your father; for One is your Father, He who is in heaven" (Matthew 23:9, NKJV).

God the Father is the creator of the heavens, the earth, and all living things. As a Father, He deals with us as children.[46] He does not treat us as an estranged Father. He becomes very active in our lives. God teaches, disciplines, listens, and shows us the right way to go. How does He do this? Does He open the sky and shout your name? No, although He could if He desired to do so because He is that amazing. He can operate through dreams, inner knowing, a soft voice, prophetic highlights, and other people, but most importantly and most consistently through His Word. The point is that God is not silent. He speaks, sees, hears, and feels. He can truly change us and be a Father to us if we will let Him. When you allow Him to do the work of a Father, He comes into our hearts and is faithful in maturing and caring for us.

I find that many people who have never had a father are drawn by God. The Bible has many scriptures showing that we are to care for the orphans or those missing a parent(s). He fills that void. It can also be difficult for people who have a negative view of their earthly fathers to see God in a healthy way, and so I hope that through these other points, we can come to know God as a good Father. For example, if you had a father who was very cold and punishing, you would view God in this way. If you had a father who was warm and gentle, you would view God in this way. I have had to undergo inner healing from dad wounds. It's quite possible that you may need to do the same. There were character flaws in my physical father that I associated with God. It's not that my father on Earth didn't do his best because he did. It is just that in the light of a perfect heavenly Father, all earthly representations will fall short.

There were many times when Jesus referred to God the Father, which consistently affirmed His identity. He understood that from this position of sonship, all of His confidence, assurance, and authority rested. In fact, it was the first thing that needed to be made known publicly before any miracle was ever performed. When Jesus was baptized, the heavens opened, and He was declared a Son. God wants us to know we are His children, and rest assured that we will never be forgotten by Him. When we understand God as Father, we can allow Him to affirm our identity, the purpose He has planned for us, and the plan to make it all happen. For extra reading, study the parable of the prodigal son in Luke 15:11–32. The parable tells us more about God's character as a loving Father that will accept back His children who may have gone astray. God's father-like heart is best reflected in this parable, ready to embrace us with open arms and a lot of love!

If you need to separate the views of your physical father from God the Father, start with this prayer:

God, I thank You that You are my Father. I thank You that You know everything about me, including the number of hairs on my head. Help me to see You as the perfect Father who is always there, who never fails and always follows through. Help me to forgive my earthly father for his failures. Please reveal to me a greater understanding of my position as Your child. I know this will be a process of healing and growing. I ask You for grace with each new level of healing. Help me to fully receive Your love as my Father. In Jesus' name, I thank You, and I pray. Amen.

### God the Righteous Judge

"There is one Lawgiver, who is able to save and to destroy. Who are you to judge another?" (James 4:12, NKJV).

God is a judge. I understand that could be a triggering concept for some people who have felt judged by imperfect people. It does not take away this aspect of God. We read earlier that God searches the hearts of man and can judge accordingly. I have often heard God being criticized as unfair. Most of my criticism toward God was rooted in viewing Him as unjust or unfair. On the contrary, God is the most just judge. I've heard on many occasions statements such as, "So you're telling me that even Hitler can be forgiven of his sin?" The truth is, yes, he could. We can't know the experience that people have at their deaths, but what we can know is that even the worst people can be forgiven. It's a hard concept for some to grab because they compare themselves to the deeds of others. If you were to compare your wrongdoing with Hitler's, you would probably look nearly perfect. The criticism comes when we compare ourselves to those who seem to be doing better than we are doing. We can't live by this double standard. Instead of viewing this in a way that is unjust, we should see that it speaks to the extent of God's mercy. If God is willing to forgive Hitler for his acts of violence, had Hitler repented, how much more do you think God is willing to forgive you? We have to understand that none are righteous before God because all have sinned.[47] I'm sure that even reading about the possibility that Hitler could be forgiven provokes some sort of reaction within you. That desire for justice, even if from our own limited understanding, is something that we share with God. A desire to see things made right.

No matter how much or how bad the sin might seem, we are all guilty of breaking God's law. God is not looking down at humanity with a scowl, just waiting to punish us. Humanity stands condemned (harshly judged) because of our own sinful nature, disobedience, and free will to act as we please. It is our flesh nature that will always choose rebellion toward God. Sin is missing the mark. It is anything that goes against the perfect nature of God. We say it all the time, "I'm not perfect." That's exactly it; none are perfect because we all fall short of the standard of God's perfection. Sin is a big deal. God hates sin because it produces evil in the world. It would be totally unjust to allow evil to go unpunished. The same anger that rises up in you when you hear a horrific news story is what God feels when He sees sin but on a greater level. We must also remember that God loves with a perfect love. God hates the very thing that destroys us, and that's sin. Sin also creates separation between God and His creation. This is why Jesus came, to close the gap of separation.

People who struggle to understand this aspect of God often claim that He is not fair. They will say something like, "It's not my fault that Adam and Eve messed up in the garden." You're absolutely right! It isn't your fault. God knows that it is not your fault and that you were born into sin. To make up for the fallen nature of man, He offered up His only Son to be a living sacrifice for you. In reality, He could have just wiped out all of humanity and started over with a brand-new Adam and Eve. He didn't do this, though. Why? Because the Father wills that not even one should perish.[48] If God were to just wipe the slate clean, Adam and Eve would have perished eternally in their fallen state. God goes a step further in showing His love and justice toward humanity. The penalty to be paid for sin is death.[49] In God's justice, He planned to send Jesus to be that payment for sin. The life of one innocent man had to legally be paid in order to purchase all of sinful humanity due to the disobedience of one couple in the Garden of Eden. When you believe in Jesus Christ, your record is essentially wiped clean, and God throws out the case of grievances against you.

The next objection often sounds like, "Why would a loving God send people to hell?" This, too, comes from an obscured view of the Father as the righteous judge. When discussing the condition of mankind, there should be more clarity concerning this objection. No matter how you try to slice it, a just God allows for punishment. It seems completely unjust to allow someone (referring back to Hitler) who caused the deaths of millions of Jews to go unpunished. Though New Age practices follow ideas such as karma to say that the person will simply return as a lesser form of a being has no justice whatsoever. Who decides what is just and unjust in the case of karma? What are the qualifications for the decisions to be made? By what moral law are those decisions made? You need a judge. Not just any judge, but one that is perfect. The only one able to judge should be one who has never been guilty of a crime. I know that God, who is the prime example of all things good and holy, is the perfect one to make this kind of judgment. We have to remember that God doesn't send anyone to hell. The truth is, we are all heading there, and we are in need of salvation. It's like waking up on a sinking boat. You wouldn't deny the reality that you were in a troubling situation but instead, look for a life raft. Jesus is that life raft.

Although many have an obscured view of God in His justice, we have to study His Word to fully understand the truths that can be revealed. God gives to each person according to their actions. Through His justice, He allows for others to get in return what they give. This is called the law of sowing and reaping.[50] This is not karma and not random chance. This is why in His fairness, He tells us, "And just as you want men to do to you, you also do to them likewise" (Luke 6:31, NKJV). This means we are to treat others the way we want to be treated. You see, at the heart of God, there is justice and fairness.

All will stand before God one day and have to give an account for the things we have done.[51] We will tell Him how we have used our time, resources, and energy. I believe we will see pieces of our life before us. There will be a day of judgment. If you have a personal relationship with God, He will deal with you as His son or daughter. If you don't personally know Jesus as Savior, you stand before Him with a record of sin. Scripture says that fear of the Lord is the beginning of all wisdom (Proverbs 9:10). I did not take God seriously before; I never had a fear of the Lord. Once you are given the fear of the Lord, something changes in your heart that allows you to respect God as the righteous judge. This isn't the type of fear you have when you watch a horror movie. It is the type of fear that means great respect. You have a revelation of the powerful nature of God, which makes surrendering and trusting His judgment much easier.

**God the Healer**

> If you diligently heed the voice of the Lord your God and do what is right in His sight, give ear to His commandments and keep all His statutes, I will put none of the diseases on you which I have brought on the Egyptians. For I am the Lord who heals you.
>
> Exodus 15:26 (NKJV)

The Bible is full of examples of healing. There are two major types of healing we see as evident in God's Word: physical and spiritual. Much of Jesus' ministry saw miracles of healing everything from leprosy to mental diseases. He was able to restore sight to the blind, bring the dead to life, and the lame could walk again. Our God is truly a healer of physical and spiritual ailments. I believe that people do get physically healed today by the power of God. I have heard countless stories of people who have been cured of cancer and seen tumors miraculously disappear. My mother is a good example of this who once had a lump appear on her ovaries, and the next visit to plan a biopsy saw that it had disappeared. Prayer certainly has the power to physically heal. God does not always heal, and we may never know why some are healing and some are not until we come face to face with Him. We do know that He works all things out according to His purpose. Job is a really great example of the type of suffering that God had planned to use for a purpose.

Spiritually, we are all in need of healing. The miracles we see Jesus perform in the New Testament all have spiritual implications. The spiritually blind are able to see when brought out of darkness into light. The dead in spirit are given new and eternal life in Christ. There are many times when we might find ourselves in compromised situations because of inner wounds that we carry. These inner wounds, which are in need of healing, might be a result of sin, abuse/trauma, or even bitterness. These things can bring disease to our soul, which is really dis-ease. We are without peace and in need of a healing touch from the Savior. Painful memories can cause us to come into agreement with lies about ourselves. Deep inner emotional wounds bring about pain stemming from bitterness. Wounds of rejection from abandonment, childhood traumas, and harboring unforgiveness lead us to act in ways of self-preservation, making it nearly impossible to place our full trust in God or to maintain healthy relationships. God wants to heal our souls so that we may find wholeness in Him. Isaiah 53:5 (NKJV) demonstrates the sacrifice of Jesus perfectly in relation to inner healing. The verse reads, "But He was wounded for our transgressions, He was bruised for our iniquities; The chastisement for our peace was upon Him, And by His stripes we are healed." We don't have to wander around, searching for the solution to our pain. He is that solution.

## God Is Perfect Love and Peace

"For God so loved the world that He gave His only begotten Son, that whoever believes in Him should not perish but have everlasting life" (John 3:16, NKJV).

Although I believe it is impossible for us to ever truly understand the depths of God's love for us, we have the Bible to tell us and our own walk as evidence. It is only through God's love and mercy that it is possible for us to have any chance at redemption.

Love is a spiritual marker of Christianity.[52] An amazing insight that God gave me early in my walk with Him was that many of His children are trapped in fear. The enemy will use fear against us. Yes, God is angry with the wicked, but aren't you? How many times have you seen the media cover stories of mass shootings, rapes, thefts, and other examples of innocent bloodshed and lives tormented? It is enough to make anyone's blood boil or hearts cry out in compassion. The same is true for God but on a greater scale because God created the very humans who are partaking in and victims of such heinous acts. Fear enslaves us. I am sure there are many times you can think about fear having a grip over your life. When I was thirteen, I began to suffer severely from sleep paralysis. If you are not familiar with sleep paralysis, it is when you are conscious of your sleep state but unable to move or speak. There are times when you'll feel intense pressure or even a choking feeling. Science has no viable explanation for this, and I read a book from a pastor telling me this was demonic oppression and to call on the name of Jesus. It worked every time. It was the sleep paralysis that made me fear the enemy and his demons.

The love of God takes away all fear, and only through His Spirit is it possible to walk in spiritual strength, which is perfected in love.[53] As followers of Christ, we should have no fear. If we believe God is who He claims to be, we understand that He walks with us and protects our souls. How is fear relevant to peace? Our souls come into perfect peace when we realize that we no longer need to fear death. The victory of Christ on the cross to conquer death was the ultimate act of love.[54] Through other scriptures, He explains that He no longer calls His disciples servants but friends and gives them a new command which is to love each other.[55] Love truly does conquer all fear. Jesus died for us so that we could be freed from the fear of death and be assured that we would be resurrected into new life. A powerful scripture that reflects this perfectly is Hebrews 2:14–15, which explains the freedom in Christ,

> Inasmuch then as the children have partaken of flesh and blood, He Himself likewise shared in the same, that through death He might destroy him who had the power of death, that is, the devil, and release those who through fear of death were all their lifetime subject to bondage.

We have a God who can empathize with the temptations that we face. He came in the form of a human and was able to experience life with all of its difficulties. No other "god" has done this, especially for the reason of wanting to save humanity, and this is the greatest act of love.

Another key component to understanding God's great love and the peace we have in Him is to know that there is no reason to fear death. You don't have to spend your entire life wondering what will happen next. God guarantees us eternal life through Jesus Christ. You do not have to be afraid of what happens after you die. In fact, we are promised to walk on streets of gold. It was God's perfect love that allowed for His plan of redemption to take place. This brings about a certain peace to our souls. Through this sacrifice, the Spirit of peace was able to enter the hearts of mankind, making salvation and walking the Christian life possible.[56] God has called us to live a life of peace. We are not able to overcome the evil of this world by fighting and devouring one another. We are called to love one another and to be at peace with all if possible for us to do so. This does not mean that you won't face trials or that you should compromise your faith. It simply means that we should not engage in a lifestyle of constant bickering, divisive behavior, or judgmental attitudes. None of those things will change a person. Only the work of the Holy Spirit has the ability to truly change a person.

**God Is Merciful**

"But go and learn what this means: 'I desire mercy and not sacrifice.' For I did not come to call the righteous, but sinners, to repentance" (Matthew 9:13).

God has never been in support of religious self-righteousness. In fact, I would venture to say that it is even downright insulting. All throughout Jesus' ministry, we see the outcast as His friend. We see the many miracles He performed, giving freedom to the ill and the possessed. He had compassion for the ones that the world had labeled useless. My tour guide in Israel explained that in Hebrew tradition, some are referred to as half-empty vessels. These were people who had not yet reached their full potential within Hebrew tradition. These were the very people that Jesus chose to sit with and teach. The ones that were put out of the synagogues and were labeled as nobodies. The Pharisees even called Jesus a glutton and a drunk because He chose to sit and speak with sinners. In fact, I would go as far as to say that He was their friend. The mercy of God was manifest throughout Jesus' ministry. He had mercy on them because He believed that He could show them a better way. It is the heart that knows it needs to change that can be impacted and not the self-righteous heart which allows no room for improvement.

I used to believe that God had one set of chosen people that He favored over everyone else. The enemy used this belief to keep me away from God and from understanding His great love toward me. I thought that I was second-rate in God's eyes because I hadn't been born a Hebrew. That is a lie from the evil one. God's mercy is for everyone, not only a select few people. Acts 10:34 (KJV) demonstrates this principle perfectly and really evens the playing field, "Then Peter opened his mouth, and said, Of a truth I perceive that God is no respecter of persons." That's good news. That means that it does not matter if you are rich, poor, old, young, male, female, black, white, Gentile, or Jew. It means that there is hope of salvation for all in the abundance of God's mercy. God sees all of creation as fallen, and we are in no position to be self-righteous because we are saved only by God's grace as every single one of us falls short of the glory of God (Romans 3:23). We don't always see things that way, though. We watch the news and see countless stories of terrible events, yet with no mercy for the one caught in the crime. Social media comments reveal much about the positioning of many hearts in difficult situations. Comments range from "throw them in jail" to "what a sick person" or "use the death penalty." It makes sense to feel that way because we seek justice. However, God calls us to a higher standard of distributing mercy to fellow human beings because His mercy toward us was perfect. No matter how much sin we've accumulated over our lives, He desires to show His mercy, which is renewed in abundance every morning.[57] Each day is a new day and a fresh start.

I am highly interested in watching court case coverage. I am usually curious about the motive of the criminal. It has often crossed my mind to consider the events that took place over the course of their lives. What had to happen throughout their life to go to such lengths and commit such atrocities? While most people instantly feel compassion toward the victim, it takes a different level of grace to consider the criminal. God's love and mercy not only comforts and heals the victim but reaches out to transform the criminal as well. I pose this question. What if it were you in that position? Wouldn't you want mercy and compassion? Thankfully, the God of the Bible is exactly that; He is merciful and compassionate. Because all have sinned, we are on the same playing field. What makes your sin any less grievous than the next person? Yet, we are typically so quick to judge when the latest scandal is smeared across the pages of a newspaper or magazine. It shouldn't be that way, but that's the world in which we live. We can all be judgmental at times, but in the end, it's only to cover up our own sin and the condition of our own hearts. We don't feel good enough when around others perceived to be better than we are, and we feel like here's when we can agree on the flaws of another. When we find someone we think is worse than ourselves, then we don't feel so badly for the things we've done or said. We must not compare ourselves to others but recognize that we are all in need of God's mercy to be made right with Him. We must follow Christ in choosing mercy over punishment.

## God Is Holy

> For thus says the High and Lofty One Who inhabits eternity, whose name is Holy: "I dwell in the high and holy place, With him who has a contrite and humble spirit, To revive the spirit of the humble, And to revive the heart of the contrite ones."

> Isaiah 57:15 (NKJV)

I believe this is a truth concerning God that we often forget. God is holy. He is the utmost perfection of all things good. If you have ever felt the presence of God, it is a feeling incomparable to any other. It is the perfection of love, peace, joy, and holiness. In His presence is no evil thing. When we look at the world around us, we see the ramifications of doing things to the best of our human ability. We may see technological or medicinal advances creating the illusion that we are simplifying our lives for the betterment of society. The reality is that even in all of these successes, we've had little success in maintaining peace. In fact, we see that human nature brings about chaos and confusion. I've heard it once said that the road to hell is paved with good intentions. I'm sure that policymakers have good intentions, but in the end, someone always loses out. This is because, apart from God, our motives are often selfish at best. Manifest destiny in American history is a good example. Though the early settlers probably did believe it was their God-given right to move westward and expand in the land, it called for the annihilation of many millions of Native American tribes. This is at least the way it is taught in the classroom. Regardless of missing pieces to the historical narrative, someone always loses out. Even in all of the human striving, we cannot reach the highest level of holiness in our fallen human effort. God shares in His set apart and perfected state by gifting us with the Holy Spirit. It is through the work of the Spirit that we are empowered to live holy and set apart. Holiness is necessary for relational growth with the Lord. Hebrews 12:14 (NKJV) reads, "Pursue peace with all people, and holiness, without which no one will see the Lord." Peace and holiness go hand in hand.

I don't believe God wants anybody to be shut out of the kingdom of heaven. I used to live with a misunderstanding of God's holiness and why certain verses seemed to be aimed at keeping me out of His kingdom. The best way this concept was revealed to me is when thinking about countries in our world. Picture yourself trying to enter a new country. When filling out the application, you realize that you are considered a rebel according to that nation's laws. Do you think they would approve your application? I think of heaven in a similar way. Think of it like this. Countries have immigration laws to keep order. There is typically a vetting process where access to the country is granted or denied. Access to terrorists (rebels) would be swiftly denied. Jesus Christ is the king of a perfect and holy kingdom. Living a lifestyle of sin and not knowing Jesus is an open rebellion according to biblical standards. Why would Jesus allow rebels into His kingdom? It is kind of like a heavenly vetting process. We need to understand that if God is holy, then His kingdom will be holy. Thankfully, the Father sent Jesus to die for us, fulfilling the whole law by living a holy and perfect life. We are called to follow the Master, and Jesus Christ is the utmost example of what it means to walk in holiness. In doing that, God is able to cleanse us from our old patterns of living and teach us how to walk in a way that is pleasing to Him.[58] Sin defiles us, and our fallen state without the Spirit of God makes us rebels to the kingdom of heaven until we become born again, and only through the blood shed by Jesus Christ is that possible. When we choose to sin, we are choosing to remain in open rebellion with the kingdom of God, and we step outside of God's protective hand.

### God Is Faithful

"If we are faithless, He remains faithful; He cannot deny Himself" (2 Timothy 2:13, NKJV).

The book of Hosea is a great place to read about how we as a spiritual nation (Israel) are completely adulterous. We worship ourselves, our cell phones, our cars, our wealth, our jobs, our shows, and our music more than God. It is not difficult to begin to idolize something. Anything we put before God is essentially an idol that we worship. If it controls you, it is a god to you. Jobs are idols for a lot of people. This section is not about idolatry. It is about the faithfulness of God. Israel had backslidden from God's ways so many times, and yet God remained faithful to His people. Despite the many idols His people placed before Him, God remained committed. He had not and would not break the covenant made to Abraham. Though as the book of Hosea points out, God had been married to an adulterous nation. Adultery is an offensive sin that many relationships today encounter. When we place things before God, we engage in a type of spiritual adultery. Instead of divorcing the nation and starting over, He chooses to remain faithful and fulfill His duty as a husband to the people. We cannot even begin to understand the faithfulness of God toward His children. Though hard times may come, God always provides a way in which we are able to escape in that our faith may become stronger.[59]

I can attest to this truth in my life. As you read at the beginning of the book, I was a prodigal child. I had walked away from the faith, and one of the first things God showed me when receiving the baptism of the Spirit was that I was never left alone. The words of Deuteronomy 31:6 rang in my ears, "Be strong and of good courage, do not fear nor be afraid of them; for the Lord your God, He is the One who goes with you. He will not leave you nor forsake you." The entire time I was in my backslidden state, God was by my side, trying to woo me as the adulterous bride I had become. Why? Because when I chose to put my faith into Jesus Christ and ask God to take control of my life, He accepted me as His child. God promises not to turn away those who will come to Him. I was in desperate need of some spiritual intervention, though. It was when I had finally come to the end of myself and trying to do it on my own that God intervened mightily to claim the possession (me) which He had bought on the cross over 2,000 years ago. God will remain faithful to you. This is not an excuse to live a lifestyle that is displeasing to Him, and I certainly would not condone being comfortable in a backslidden state. I would, however, say that it speaks to the true nature of God, which is that even when we fail Him, He is waiting there with open arms, ready to receive us into His love. We need not be afraid of the world or our circumstances because we have a faithful God who cannot forget His children.[60]

### God Has a Will

"Not everyone who says to Me, 'Lord, Lord,' shall enter the kingdom of heaven, but he who does the will of My Father in heaven" (Matthew 7:21, NKJV).

There are many scriptures that point out that those who belong to Jesus Christ are those who do the will of the Father. God's will for each of our individual lives in terms of purpose is a lifelong process of following Him in obedience to fulfill the plan He has for each of us. In a way, Proverbs 25:2 (KJV) makes a lot of sense here, "It is the glory of God to conceal a thing: But the honour of kings is to search out a matter." Can you imagine if God just told you about His entire plan for your life? You would probably try everything in your own power to make it happen. When we seek God, we are able to walk in the steps He has ordered for our lives.[61] Along the way will be many trials, all of which will test and grow our faith.

God also has a more well-known will. Let's take a look at what the Father wills for each of His children. John 6:40 (NKJV) tells us, "And this is the will of Him who sent Me, that everyone who sees the Son and believes in Him may have everlasting life; and I will raise him up at the last day." This reveals so much about the heart of God. He is not an unfair tyrant that seeks utter destruction. He is a righteous judge that has mercy upon a fallen creation. He sees a world of iniquity but looks upon us with love so great that He sent His only Son to be a sacrifice for us. A love so deep that we would not have to partake in eternal punishment, though we have all broken God's law. This is only possible by having faith in Jesus Christ. As stated in John 6:40, we have learned that the Father wills for us to have faith in the Son.[62] Through this faith, we come into a personal relationship. John 6:39 shows us that He pursues us with an unceasing love. Even when we, like sheep, have gone astray, the power of God is greater than our own weakness. The verse reads, "This is the will of the Father who sent Me, that of all He has given Me I should lose nothing, but should raise it up at the last day" (NKJV). When we understand God's will for our lives, we can connect on a deeper level with His heart toward us. God is faithful to us, even when we have failed Him.

This does not take away the fact that we are called to holiness. An often-overlooked scripture in today's world is 1 Thessalonians 4:3–5, which describes another part of God's will:

> For this is the will of God, your sanctification: that you should abstain from sexual immorality; that each of you should know how to possess his own vessel in sanctification and honor, not in passion of lust, like the Gentiles who do not know God.

We are to consistently seek out God's will for our lives both personally and with the understanding that we should be heading for Christ-likeness.[63] God forgives and has grace for our shortcomings, but God also wills for our sanctification. A process of the purification of the heart which allows for us to bear good fruit.

In short, the will of God for our personal lives is something that is revealed over time through prayer and individual relationships. God's will for all humanity is salvation and sanctification. This is made possible through faith by believing in Jesus (salvation) and the sanctification of your soul through the washing of the Word. The Word of God should be something that transforms every aspect of your life. By living in such a way and through faith, we can trust that we are within the will of God. This makes praying "Your will be done" a little more understandable (Matthew 6:10). We must position our hearts to seek God about His personal will for our lives.

**God Has a Plan**

"Trust in the Lord with all your heart, And lean not on your own understanding; In all your ways acknowledge Him, And He shall direct your paths" (Proverbs 3:5–6, NKJV).

God has a plan for your life. Remember that it is the glory of kings to search out a matter. If David had not been obedient to God by placing his trust in Him, he would not have slain the giant Goliath. If Joseph had not kept faith when he was sold into slavery by his brothers, God could not have exalted him as king over Egypt. Had Esther remained silent, she would not have seen freedom for her people as queen. We have to remember that God has a plan even in the midst of adversity. If you are seeking God's plan for your life, know that it will always be better than you could have ever imagined. God has our best interest at heart, "And we know that in all things God works for the good of those who love him, who have been called according to his purpose" (Romans 8:28, NIV). We are assured of God's thoughts toward us in Jeremiah 29:11 (NKJV), "For I know the thoughts that I think toward you, says the Lord, thoughts of peace and not of evil, to give you a future and a hope." This reveals just how valuable you are to God and how He is willing and able to use each and every one of us. All Christians play a vital role in the body of Christ. You were created for much more than you could have ever dreamed for yourself.

**Final Thoughts on God's Character**

We have not even begun to unravel the full nature of God. There is so much more that we could speak about. I feel it is impossible to ever fully understand God. When He makes Himself known through the Holy Spirit, He will lead you into understanding concerning His Word. Go into depth with God when you pray privately. Ask Him to reveal more of Himself to you because you want to get to know Him. He never disappoints. When I sought God to know more about His character, He led me to Nehemiah 9:18–21 (NKJV):

> Even when they made a molded calf for themselves, And said, "This is your god That brought you up out of Egypt," And worked great provocations, Yet in Your manifold mercies You did not forsake them in the wilderness. The pillar of the cloud did not depart from them by day, To lead them on the road; Nor the pillar of fire by night, To show them light, And the way they should go. You also gave Your good Spirit to instruct them, And did not withhold Your manna from their mouth, And gave them water for their thirst. Forty years You sustained them in the wilderness; They lacked nothing; Their clothes did not wear out And their feet did not swell.

In my darkest moments, I lean on these scriptures to remind myself of God's character, which is important in combatting the lies of the enemy. In this one passage, we see His mercy, grace, love, patience, provision, and faithfulness. The enemy tries to manipulate us by attempting to get us to see God in a way that is a lie. This is why I will again stress the importance of having a right view of God shaped by the truths revealed about Him in the Bible. That does not mean that you won't have to become aware of and eventually let go of the wrong ideas we hold about God. When we go through this process of discovery, we begin to learn more about ourselves and the God who created us. You can begin the process by asking yourself some simple questions, like who is God to you? What do you believe God thinks about you? What do you believe about God, and when did you learn that about Him? I often find that we need to unlearn whatever does not align with the consistent picture of His character created in the Bible and relearn Him according to His Word. When we read scriptures that paint God out to be an evil, unfair, judgmental tyrant, then we need to recognize that something in our understanding of that scripture is lacking. We must be anchored in the truth that God is always good, loving, merciful, faithful, and just. It is through a right understanding of God and a deeper relationship with Him that we learn more about ourselves so that we can walk boldly into the plans and purposes He has for each and every one of us.

# Set Apart

> But you are a chosen generation, a royal priesthood, a holy nation, His own special people, that you may proclaim the praises of Him who called you out of darkness into His marvelous light.
>
> 1 Peter 2:9 (NKJV)

As a follower of Christ, you will stand out. You have not been called to the many paths but to one path set apart, which is Jesus. Diversity and inclusion are important, but it is vital not to forsake your faith for the sake of inclusion. If we can understand the truth of our set-apart nature as children of God, we can feel greater confidence to avoid conforming to what the larger group deems as acceptable. God has called us out of the world. He has changed us. This means that you are going to be at odds with the thinking pattern of the world. Satan's job is to keep people hating and fighting with each other. We can see this through the extremely biased media outlets, which will portray the same story in two different ways. The idea is to divide and conquer. If you can divide the people, you can maintain power over them. The stark split on social issues has bred hatred in the hearts of many. When the enemy is successful, our world is filled with chaos, confusion, and fear. If you have hatred in your heart toward any person or group of people, then you are not acting according to God's love. We have not been called to judge the world. We have been called to be set apart from it and to shine as bright lights. Our lives are a living testimony of the power of God.

A life that forsakes sin and brings ourselves into alignment with God's will. Sin is destructive, and we must understand that people are broken, hurting souls in need of a Savior. We don't do our peers any favors by changing our faith to make them more comfortable. Instead, we should help navigate the issue through lenses of grace and understanding. The world is in desperate need of the love of God to fill their hearts. Find joy in the fact that though you may be rejected by the world, you are accepted by God.

Schools love to compartmentalize. The subjects are broken up into different departments, which makes big picture learning more difficult as students strive to see the connections in the world but instead see these subjects as separate. The same is true for a student's interests. There will typically be some sort of club fair that serves a student's interests but also separates them. There are different groups or teams you can join, and with each comes a pre-conceived idea about who you are if you join them. This is where false identities can be formed, and it is important to separate what you do from who you are. It can feel a bit unsettling when making a choice as to where to go. Cue the mini identity crisis that takes place as you try to figure out where you belong. The affiliations we make with friends at this time can become another key marker in identity. I remember joining the club fair the first week of my freshman year of college. I was nervous about making a choice. There were sororities, sports teams, interest clubs, and even a Christian club. I am sad to say that I bypassed the group with Christian representation, but at the time, I didn't want to be identified in this way. Church was something I occasionally did and wasn't a large part of who I was at the time. I didn't want to continue on the cheer team. I did that in high school and felt a lack of fulfillment and slight bitterness for how my senior year ended. Instead, I went to the drama club. I have always loved theater and the arts and felt this was a chance to learn. God has a funny way of preparing you for things you'll do later in life. Ten years later, I had the opportunity to write and direct an original play for my church which resulted in lives being given to Jesus. As much as I loved my theater troupe, they didn't bring me closer to the Lord. In fact, there were times I had to do or say certain things that I was not comfortable with for the sake of the production. I do not want to discourage you from pursuing your God-given talents during this time. I do hope that you will use wisdom and trust that if God gave you the gift, He will lead in how it should be used. If I could do something differently, I would go back and also surround myself with people that I knew would bring me closer to God.

If you see a lack of Christian representation in your school and are feeling bold, start a Christian club. Most schools allow students to start their own groups if they can show a desire for its presence. That usually means getting a few others to sign up with you. If joining a Christian community is not an option, pray that God will lead you to a Christian fellowship group. Some college campuses have different organizations that are connected to this sort of thing. The Christian walk is not easy, and fellowship with other believers is important for your growth. Another great thing to involve yourself in is community service. It's an amazing way to display your faith as you serve others.

Keep yourself busy, but not too busy to do God's work. Avoid the frat/sorority parties that center around drinking, or post-sporting event keg parties, dorm parties, and so on. I have seen people get taken advantage of during events like this. Some have been kicked out of school, and others have even been arrested. I am not saying you can't have fun, but being set apart also means living in a way that is reflective of the lifestyle of Jesus. Typically, churches create youth events that allow for you to have just as much fun in a way that won't encourage you to behave in a way that you know you wouldn't if your pastor was present. That does not mean you won't make mistakes, but acknowledging that our identity is not found within our social groups.

The people you surround yourself with become a type of personal identity. Our differences are front and center when on campus. They are looked at as being something that places us into groups based on similarities. When we seek to reach others, we should be focused on what makes us human. If we could focus on our similarities, we would have far less division and contention. What do we focus on? We all want to be loved. We all want to succeed. We all have questions about life. We have all been through something that may have hurt us. The bottom line is that we have more in common than we know. First Corinthians 9:19–22 (NKJV) explains this very well,

> For though I am free from all men, I have made myself a
> servant to all, that I might win the more; and to the Jews
> I became as a Jew, that I might win Jews; to those who are

under the law, as under the law, that I might win those
who are under the law; to those who are without law, as
without law (not being without law toward God, but
under law toward Christ), that I might win those who are
without law; to the weak I became as weak, that I might
win the weak. I have become all things to all men, that I
might by all means save some.

We need to be able to relate to people while also understanding
that God has marked us as His. This means your experiences won't be
average. They will be different. You are called to a different path. A
path that is narrow. This means that you'll do things differently than
the way others do them. Yet we must seek to understand others so
that we can connect with them in the ways that matter. Paul made it
a point in his evangelistic efforts to meet people where they were for
the sake of spreading the gospel.

After laying some foundational truths, you should now be more
well equipped to speak the truth concerning the faith in a way that is
easy to understand. To be a Christian is not an easy thing, but with
God on our side, nothing is impossible. Part two is going to deal with
the way in which the education system has been designed around
producing faithless students. Really I should say students who have
put their faith into the world and not in God. Students who may
have been brought up in the faith are challenged heavily during this
time, and it can seem overwhelming if you are not prepared. Part two
will serve to explore some of those challenges as well as how you can

overcome them and be a witness for the faith in the classroom.

## Called to the Classroom

For the message of the cross is foolishness to those who
are perishing, but to us who are being saved it is the power
of God.

1 Corinthians 1:18 (NKJV)

The Greeks had a meeting place known as the Agora. This was
an assembly through which they would discuss politics, philosophy,
and other ideas. The modern classroom often engages in a similar
fashion referred to as Socratic seminars. There is usually a chance
for open dialogue. The issue of intense social pressure causes those
with an unpopular opinion to conform to the general consensus for
a few reasons. Typically one may feel unsure that their opinion is
the "correct" one. Another reason is fear of social isolation, which
often results in negative labels or may be cited as hate speech. Some
may just have a fear of stating their opinion or speaking openly in
public. When these things are mixed together, it can create an
almost dictatorial environment that fosters one commonly believed
narrative. The popular opinion in these situations is typically not the
one for Jesus Christ. I remember a specific example of working with
seventh-graders. We sat in a circle and shared our thoughts about
various discussion prompts. I remember the tension in the room
becoming very thick when one student mentioned their Bible was
very important to them and a treasured possession. Some students
laughed, and others looked at me with an expression of "Is that
okay to say?" I spoke to the students' parents at a parent-teacher

conference and asked permission to encourage their child in the faith. I remember telling this student to hold fast to what he believes and to continue to walk in the way he's been called. To not change his answer because others may think it's funny. A similar situation occurred with a student of another faith. This time the room was filled with compassion, and the student was celebrated for his bravery. I am not a huge fan of double standards. All of that is to say that it's important to have the right tools in your toolbox for situations like the ones mentioned above. Here are eight tips for how to navigate those kinds of situations.

### Tip #1: Know When to Speak

Ask God to lead you concerning when to speak. Sometimes we are led not to speak, and this could give God an opportunity to work on the hearts of our classmates and professors. James 1:19 (NKJV) highlights this perfectly for us, "So then, my beloved brethren, let every man be swift to hear, slow to speak, slow to wrath." Knowing when to speak is imperative for success. Listening to the points of others around you gives you an opportunity to really think about what you are going to say. Is it beneficial? Could it be taken the wrong way? How can I word it in a way that will bring light to the situation? I used to be the type of person to speak very quickly and quite often within the classroom. Participation is a good thing, but I have learned a more effective way. When you listen more than you speak, those around you are more likely to pay closer attention when you do share your voice. It is kind of like that one kid in class that rarely speaks, and when they do, everyone is in shock and listens closely to what they have to say. I am certainly not saying don't participate, but I am saying know when to share and know when to reserve your comments. There have been times when I wanted to defend a point, but it could have given way to anger. Just as the verse in James says, be slow to wrath. It is no surprise that this verse has three main points: listen, speak, and don't give way to anger. In the midst of hot-button issues, it isn't hard to want to speak over someone to get your point across, and then they respond back with an attitude because they're offended, so you try to defend yourself, and then suddenly you're yelling at each other. Remain calm and hear what people have to say. Give a well-constructed response and move forward. I don't want to see you become discouraged if attacked by other classmates for having a viewpoint that is contrary to the norm. God knows the condition of each heart in that classroom, including your own. Do not be afraid to speak, but ask God for the right words. There is power in your tongue, and our words carry a lot of weight. Ask God to increase your boldness if you are shy. If you have no problem speaking your mind, ask God to show you how to do this in love.[64]

### Tip #2: Ask God for Wise Words

Debates can and do happen in the classroom. It can get heated, especially if the teacher lets the discussion carry on longer than it should. Many teachers and professors today are fairly open with their personal biases. I remember doing a teacher observation when starting my job at the middle school. They were doing a project on social justice issues. The seventh-grade girl was against abortion and wanted to write about that. The teacher showed shock that she would have this viewpoint. The teacher egged her on and said, "What if the baby was a result of rape?" The student looked confused and said, "Well, I guess it's okay if that happens." The teacher later backpedaled and said, "Of course, it's your opinion. I am just giving you another view." Not only was that completely inappropriate, but it wouldn't be the conversation had the student been in favor of abortion. She would have been encouraged to strengthen her viewpoint with facts rather than question and doubt her stance. This is why we need to not only be firm in what we believe but in why we believe it. I also encourage bringing a situation like the one mentioned above to a trusted spiritual mentor who can give you a biblically rooted response. God just may want to work through you to bring light into darkness.

You don't have to defend God. His Word speaks for itself. The Word of God is truth, and it is life. It is a powerful weapon for warfare, and speaking it out loud can pierce the hearts of the listener. Hebrews 4:12 (NKJV) demonstrates the power of the Word,

> For the word of God is living and powerful, and sharper than any two-edged sword, piercing even to the division of soul and spirit, and of joints and marrow, and is a discerner of the thoughts and intents of the heart.

At times, this means speaking the Word of God into a situation. Other times, it means consulting the Word when situations take place that leaves us perplexed, like that of the seventh-grader and her social justice project. Do not forget that God's Word has the ability to change and transform lives. God may use this time to push you out of your comfort zone. Every situation will be different. The Bible provides wisdom through which we are able to understand people a bit better. Perhaps they are bitter, depressed, defensive, or angry in class. When we are grounded in the Word of God, we are better able to understand a little bit about why a person may be reacting to us in this way. The condition of the heart of each listener will vary. Seek God's wisdom concerning how to proceed in each case, and do not fear. You were placed where you are for such a time as this.

### Tip #3: Know You Have the Truth

There will always be some sort of gap in the logic of those not led by God. Remember that the enemy can only mimic what God has created. The enemy will serve you a lie with a piece of truth. In fact, the best lies are 90 percent true. We tend to identify with the stolen piece of truth, yet the lie is what goes over our heads. He does this by first causing us to doubt what God says is true and then providing his lie as truth. Genesis 3:4 (NKJV) shows this tactic, "Then the serpent said to the woman, 'You will not surely die. For God knows that in the day you eat of it your eyes will be opened, and you will be like God, knowing good and evil.'" God did say they would die if they ate of that tree, and it is true that their eyes would be opened. We can identify both the lie and the stolen truth.

I had spent a lot of time under the delusion of reincarnation. I remember having a conversation with my dad, and he asked, "How can you work your way back up the chain if you're an ant?" This was something I couldn't answer. There is no answer. It goes against the laws that are implied by karma. An ant is not a being that has the decision to choose right and wrong. There are no good works the ant can do to gain good karma to move up the chain to a mammal of some sort. My dad found the gap in logic. A major reason why I do suggest studying other belief systems with the understanding that they are works-based is that it better equips you to understand why people believe the things they do. When you are firmly grounded in the truth, finding faulty reasoning becomes quite easy. I like to use the buddha as a great example. Siddhartha Gautama set out to understand suffering and find a way of alleviating himself from it. The problem is that his teachings only brought more suffering upon himself in his attempt to find freedom. These little facts are very helpful when discussing different belief systems, and you will learn about them in class.

What I have noticed is that most people are essentially searching for truth. They regurgitate information learned from others and sometimes tend to be open to a change in their belief system. Though this is not always the case, as belief systems for some have become a core part of their identity, such as the case within some families. It is strongly discouraged to learn about other beliefs in some cultures, which results in a level of fear of exploring other faiths. This could mean being ostracized from their family, friends, and other social circles. I had a Muslim student ask me a question about Jesus once, and he was so nervous he began to sweat. He feared being sent to hell for even asking. When you are interacting with various people, you must carry compassion toward the issues a person might face. For some people, becoming a Christian truly means losing everything. When you show someone you care for them, it lowers their defenses, making it possible for them to receive you more warmly. The majority of the people that I have had the opportunity to interact with were open to hearing new ideas. In my experience, a majority of my peers had some idea about Christianity, both good and bad. Thankfully, God has given us the truth in His Word to be able to test all things according to what we are being taught. You may just be that voice of logic and truth that God wants to use to bring light to the class. There will be times when your faith in God's Word will be tested. The enemy will stop at nothing to get you to doubt that what God says is true. Keep the mindset that the Bible is truth, and you can test all other claims according to what the Word reveals.

### Tip #4: Prepare to Be a Minority Voice

Do not give up if you feel like the only voice crying out in the wilderness. You may feel like an outsider. There will probably be a strong pressure to conform to what others are doing. The secular world contrasts directly with God's truth, and this will set you apart. People cannot understand the profound truths that God reveals in His Word with the rational mind because it goes against what we have been conditioned to believe to be true according to the world.[65] We have an immense desire to fit in and be accepted by those around us. Nobody wants to feel like the odd one out that the world has rejected. This is why having your identity firmly established in Christ is so important. What does the Word of God say about you? You have not been rejected. You are not a loser for being different. God loves the outcast. Deuteronomy 14:2 (NKJV) says, "For you are a holy people to the Lord your God, and the Lord has chosen you to be a people for Himself, a special treasure above all the peoples who are on the face of the earth." We are pilgrims sojourning through this world, but we have been transformed by the power of God and can no longer be accepted by the world because we do not conform to its ways. We quickly learn that the path in which the world is taking is leading straight to destruction.[66] The world has rejected you because God has accepted you.

Social pressure led to my biggest downfall during my school years. I wanted to fit in so badly that I slowly began to compromise. I was tired of being called "the Jesus girl." Little compromises became big compromises. Sin kind of works that way. You may know you're doing something wrong, but the more you do it, the quieter that voice of conviction gets and the easier the offense becomes. Moral truths I once thought to be true came into question. I thought maybe I was wrong because look at what everybody else was doing. I began to believe lie after lie until, eventually, I had no idea what to believe. The enemy leads you down a slippery slope of deception. Social pressure is probably the number one tool the enemy will use to silence you. This is why people-pleasing will only distance you from serving God fully. We should seek to please God and not people. When we seek to please people, we may compromise the truth. God will go before you, so do not be afraid to speak the truth in boldness with love and seasoned with salt.[67]

### Tip #5: Know That People Want to Hear Your Opinion

You may be familiar with this unspoken and sometimes spoken belief that you must remain silent about your faith. People will emphasize that we are all entitled to our own beliefs, and we should keep them to ourselves. This is a tool the enemy tries to use to discourage Christians from evangelizing. If you have been discouraged with thoughts that nobody will listen or that nobody cares, I am here to tell you that is a lie. People are hurting. There is a world full of people who are in desperate need of hearing the gospel of Jesus Christ. Romans 1:16 (NKJV) says it best, "For I am not ashamed of the gospel of Christ, for it is the power of God to salvation for everyone who believes." Not only do you have the words that people need to hear for eternal salvation, but you can see souls being set free from lifelong bondages. We have to ask ourselves. What makes our good deeds and the words we speak any different from the rest of the world? The rest of the world can speak positive affirmations, meditate on good things, and give to the poor. When we speak the truth of God's Word, we introduce them to Jesus. Where mindful meditation fails, the Holy Spirit's lifelong guidance prevails. Schools today love integrating practices like yoga and mindful meditation. Although they may not know the esoteric roots of such practices, they are introducing methods to students as young as kindergarten as a way to manage stress and anxiety. We have something that is lasting and not temporary. Where bread given to the poor is temporary, a relationship with Jesus Christ lasts forever. The witness you carry in testifying to the truth of His power will be your motivation to focus on concerning the belief that nobody will listen or cares what you have to say. Then you won't feel pressured to share with others. You may not realize it, but people do listen. Seeds are being planted in the hearts of those around you, and everything is revealed in its proper time. You may not see the fruits of your labor right away. You may not know the impact until you see Jesus face to face, but that does not mean that what you say does not or will not impact those around you.

**Tip #6: Know Your Rights**

You have a right to speak freely about your faith. Schools practice open discussion. Public schools are government-run institutions, and the battle for religious free speech is a little more difficult. It is important to know that you still have the right to speak freely and openly about Jesus. I say this because I do not want you to be discouraged from speaking. Legally, you have the right to free speech and religious freedom. This includes not allowing anybody to discourage you or stop you from praying. The biggest attack concerning public schools was with the late Madalyn Murray O'Hair, who had Christian practices such as prayer banned from school. This does not mean that you cannot pray or speak to others about your faith. A school cannot hinder most religious practices. I had three Muslim students who would leave class every day around 1 p.m. to pray for fifteen minutes. We had to grant them this time, or else we would be infringing on their right to practice their religion. There were also special accommodations made for these students during times of fasting around certain holidays. Many schools will go to great lengths to make these accommodations, and you, too, can request something reasonable if need be. Do not feel bullied into thinking you must compromise your values. Stand firmly on the rock that is Christ, and He will make a way. He did it for Daniel when the decree was sent out that it would be illegal to pray, and He will do it for you too.

**Tip #7: Be Honest With Your Teachers/Professors**

Honesty truly is the best policy. There might be an occasion where something said during class or the content being taught may make you uncomfortable. Schools today are consistently pushing the boundaries between what is and what is not appropriate for classroom discussion. This will often hinge on three things: your teacher, your classmates, and the course curriculum. I had professors that would let us walk out of the classroom for a while if something we were discussing was extremely controversial. If I recall correctly, my history and sociology classes were typically the ones that were the most controversial. Perhaps something said has made you feel uncomfortable, and you don't want to walk out of the room. Meeting with the teacher or professor after class or during office hours to discuss the situation is always an option. In some cases, you can even request an alternative curriculum. I have seen this happen to

Jehovah's Witness students whose parents did not want them to read a story about magic.

Teachers and professors are called to be professional and unbiased. This is not always the case, but it is worth the effort to approach them. In the event that the content you are learning leads to a bigger project or paper, some teachers/professors will be understanding and may offer you a writing or project alternative. A fair amount of the humanities courses allow for some level of leniency concerning course readings and various writing that you will produce. I used my master's classes as a way to learn more about God. When the opportunity presented itself, I would choose books or time periods pertaining to the faith. An example of this was during my History of English class. I decided to write my term paper on the impact the Kings James Bible had on the English language. Although I never formally attended any seminary school, I used every opportunity to grow in this way, given the circumstances. In an extreme circumstance, where you genuinely felt singled out or treated differently for being a Christian, you can report a complaint to the department chair. If you feel that you earned a grade wrongfully, you can fight your grade. The sad truth is that this can happen. When writing my master's thesis, I took a course on research. The professor continuously gave me negative feedback because my compilation of texts and explanation of the choices reinforced an idea on which we did not agree. I argued that a worldwide flood most likely did take place based on the worldwide influence of texts recounting very similar variations of the story. He believed it to only be a myth, and so I was graded accordingly. Ultimately, I scored well in the class, but I think this was God's grace because this guy did not like me very much. In any case, do not compromise the truth of your faith for an A. God will always work out each situation to your benefit.

**Tip #8: Pray Before Class**

Praying before each class is a practice that I adopted in graduate school. It eventually turned into a really good habit. I would get to class early and even anoint the desks. I used my God-given authority in Christ to come against any assignment of the enemy to blind the minds of those in the room. I asked God to send angels to war with the enemy while the class took place. I prayed for protection for myself and others in the class. Ephesians 6:12 reminds us, "For we do not wrestle against flesh and blood, but against ...powers, against the rulers of the darkness of this age, against spiritual hosts of wickedness in the heavenly places." This means that as a child of God, you are given authority through Christ over the rulers of darkness. You have the power of prayer to back you up before every class. If you are the type of person that is normally late to class, this is a good practice to help you to be on time. If you are the first one in the room, you can make your declarations and pray out loud. Staying in constant prayer is key, and it is a practice with which many Christians struggle. You can do this, and God will bring others along the way. When you pray, ask God to soften the hearts of those around you so that you can plant a seed. I will give an example of how this has happened in my own life. I prayed that God would give me an opportunity to speak about Him with one of my peers. That same day, I walked into the school library to take out some books for a research project. There was a young man working behind the counter who had a shirt on that said something about love. Here comes the still, small voice, "Tell him I love him." My response was, "What, really?" So I asked for strength and boldness at that moment and said, "Hey, cool shirt. Did you know that Jesus loves you?" He proceeded to tell me that was the third time he heard that this week. Fair enough to say that he was intrigued by this strange occurrence, and we have had several discussions concerning faith since. The bottom line is that God answers prayers.

## The Classroom Disciple

He who says he abides in Him ought himself also to walk just as He walked.

1 John 2:6 (NKJV)

What does it mean to be a disciple of Christ? How do you navigate discipleship in the classroom, which claims to be unbiased in the religious sense? All of this first stems from gaining a firm grasp on what it means to follow Christ. Then we can be better prepared for any obstacle we will encounter. There are four main markers of a disciple of Christ. Those markers are love, humility, suffering, and service.

## The Disciple Who Loves

The Bible is clear that one way to recognize someone who is a disciple of Christ is by their love.[68] The apostle Paul stresses the importance of love in his letter to the church in Corinth:

> Though I speak with the tongues of men and of angels, but have not love, I have become sounding brass or a clanging cymbal. And though I have the gift of prophecy, and understand all mysteries and all knowledge, and though I have all faith, so that I could remove mountains, but have not love, I am nothing. And though I bestow all my goods to feed the poor, and though I give my body to be burned, but have not love, it profits me nothing.
>
> 1 Corinthians 13:1–3 (NKJV)

Paul shows us that we can have every spiritual gift, a lot of faith, and even be a martyr, but without love, it is all pointless. Love needs to be deeply anchored within our souls. How can you truly represent Jesus if you're yelling to get your point across? Perhaps a debate in class gets heated, and now you are triggered and thinking some pretty mean thoughts. We cannot carry an attitude of looking down on the lost or acting as if we are better than others. Jesus never did this. The Pharisees did. The people who chose to follow Jesus followed Him because of mercy, kindness, and grace, which is impossible to exhibit without love. Jesus specifically reached for the outcasts and those rejected by normal society. People are more open to hearing you if they know that you love and care for them. This means so much more than simply trying to get your point across. This behavior can even repel people and create a false view of who Christ is, adding fuel to the lies of the enemy. If you've made that mistake, there is forgiveness.

Loving someone does not mean you need to agree with everything they do. In fact, love is one of the most misused words in the English language. Many people describe love as something I once heard called fish love. This basically means that we attribute love to things that aren't even love in the first place. You may have ordered a nice fish dinner and said, "I love fish." Do you really love fish? Would you lay down your life for the fish? What you really mean is that you enjoy eating fish. You don't love fish. Love is not necessarily a feeling. Love is not what we see in romantic comedies. That is a fleeting feeling that comes and goes. We are instead commanded to love as God loves. This includes loving our enemies. I know I certainly may not feel love toward a person who openly rejects my ideas in class, but I am still called to treat them with respect. When we think of love, we have to think about service. The way that Jesus served us by dying for us while we did nothing to deserve it. We can say we love somebody, but there is truth to the age-old euphemism, "Actions speak louder than words." This is exactly what James was trying to show us by writing, "Faith without works is dead."[69] The Bible talks a lot about doing for others. Good works come as a result of a faith that is alive. Good works are not what get you into right standing with God but are a result of the Holy Spirit working in us. Jesus Christ, in an act of service and love toward His disciples, even washed their feet. That takes a lot of humility to be the Savior of the world and to wash the feet of those who follow you. He even washed the feet of Judas, who would later betray Him for thirty pieces of silver. How do you love those around you?

**The Humble Disciple**

By far, one of the most difficult lessons is to remain humble and think about the well-being of others. It can be hard because it is in direct contrast with our flesh nature. The flesh seeks to serve itself and is rooted in pride. When we seek to be a disciple of Christ, we must allow God to humble us. We must be focused on the needs of others and not making a name for ourselves. This does not mean that God won't give you favor with man in the world. It just means that our motives need to be pure. Jesus humbled Himself to the point that He never sought glory for His own name but that all glory would go to the Father.[70] We must follow in His footsteps. Human ambition can be one of the most difficult things to overcome. We all have dreams and life goals, but seeking God about the direction He wants to take you is a key to accomplishing the assignment placed on your life. God's plan for your life may look different than your plan. Our goal in life is not to make a name for ourselves so that we will be remembered. It is to point others to the only name that has the power to set people free, and that's the name of Jesus. I am not saying God will not bless you, but that we should not seek self-promotion or self-exaltation. When we have the wrong motives, we begin to build our own kingdom instead of seeking first God's kingdom.[71] When you put the needs of others before your own and seek to serve God for the promotion of His kingdom, He blesses you more than you could possibly imagine.[72] I am not saying to neglect yourself and give so much that you burn out. A lot of people make that mistake. This is more in reference to an attitude of the heart. Serving others using your God-given gifts and talents is not only a blessing for yourself but for others. We exhibit humility and selflessness when we use the things God has blessed us with to be a blessing to others. In serving them, we exhibit sacrificial love.

### A Disciple That Suffers

Unfortunately, we don't speak enough about suffering. The truth is that we have and will continue to encounter obstacles throughout our lives. Jesus warned the disciples that they would encounter tough times, but His peace was available to them.[73] Everyone will suffer at some point in life. Though I cannot claim to have all of the answers concerning this world and suffering, I can make a few biblical observations. I want to be 100 percent honest with you about this topic. I don't want to set you up to falsely believe that following Jesus means a walk in the park on a sunny day. It doesn't mean that at all. Jesus made this clear when people inquired about following Him. In Matthew 8:20, Jesus explains that being His disciple is not always so glamorous. The text reads, "Foxes have holes, and the birds of the air have nests, but the Son of Man has no place to lay His head" (paraphrased by the author). You may not always know the next step, but just like God led the Israelites into the wilderness as preparation for the inheritance of the promised land, you will be led into and through difficult times in your life. Why does following Christ mean there will be no full eradication of suffering? The end of suffering does not come in full until the establishment of the new heaven and the new earth.[74] This present world, because of its fallen and sinful nature, makes room for evil and suffering. Everything that the enemy uses for evil to try to hurt us, God will turn around to grow us and mold our character. To do a deeper study on Christian suffering, the book of Job is a great place to start.

God will use the hardships we encounter throughout life to be a blessing to others. There is a certain level of compassion that is produced when we can relate to the pains of others. The major difference is how we deal with a crisis. When the world encounters turmoil, they have few options to turn to for support. As a Christian, you have a God that tells you nothing is impossible. There is no crisis too big for God to turn around. In short, we have hope which is made available to us through faith in Christ.[75] We are given a certain peace of mind that the rest of the world does not have. Hardships allow for the refining of our faith. Please do not be discouraged if you find yourself in a tough situation. Trust that God will bring you through it, and there will be a purpose for it. God turns all things around for our good. When we encounter tough times in our life and rely solely on God, we set an example for those around us. People view us as being followers of Christ, and they watch how we will respond to these types of situations. When we walk in faith, allowing God to carry us every step of the way, we give glory to the Father. When people go through situations that seem impossible to overcome in human strength, God is given an opportunity to show His power, glory, faithfulness, and love.

## A Disciple of Service

We are called to serve others. There are many ways through which we are able to serve those around us. You could take the traditional route and volunteer for some community service opportunities. Maybe you don't have a lot of time to give or want to know how you can serve others daily. What I have found to be the most fulfilling is passing on a small act of kindness. This is a great way to show that you are a disciple of Christ. It gives you an opportunity to say something as simple as "God bless you." In our world today, very rarely will you see someone go out of their way to do something kind for someone else, let alone see much social interaction that isn't electronic. Jesus made it clear that we are to do kind things for other people. The pattern of the world does not follow this as it is inherently self-seeking. When we serve others, we act selflessly by putting their needs before our own. Jesus said it best in Matthew 5:41–42 (NKJV), "And whoever compels you to go one mile, go with him two. Give to him who asks you, and from him who wants to borrow from you do not turn away." A mile goes a long way in the hearts of those around us who are not used to being given even an inch.

What could the small act of kindness look like? It could mean offering your seat to someone who needs it more in the packed-out library. It could be helping someone carry their books or opening the door when you see that they are struggling. It could be staying for a minute after class to see if your stressed-out professor could use your help with anything. Maybe it means sitting with someone who is all alone in the cafeteria. Little things like this set us apart from others. When we seek to serve others above ourselves, a person is more readily willing to hear what you have to say, making it much easier to share your faith. Make friends by building bridges that lead them to the one who made them.

Sharing your faith can be difficult. When we follow the teachings of Jesus, we show the person that we care about them. When we show others that we are willing to help them out and hear what they have to say, a level of trust begins to build. Little opportunities such as this are simple ways to begin a conversation and let people know that there is a God who loves them, cares about them, and has a plan for their lives. It just takes a little bit of boldness. When you speak to others, do not be ashamed or fear what they will think or say. Instead, show them you care through a small act of kindness which can open the door to a deeper conversation. People are hurting. They need to hear about Jesus. Who will tell them if not you?

A practical way to begin a conversation is by finding common ground. I have been blessed with a level of boldness. I can walk right up to somebody and say, "Jesus loves you." Not everyone is like that. I wasn't always like that. God had worked in me to build my confidence and self-esteem. There are days when that is hard for me to do, but I recognize that a missed opportunity only leads to regret. I have learned that discipleship isn't really about me but about representing Christ in me. You might be asking, how do I start the conversation? A random act of kindness is always a good place to start. It gives you an opening to share your faith. For example, midterms or finals could be quickly approaching. This is typically a high-stress period for college students. The Bible has a lot of great advice concerning worry. I remember speaking to someone who was so stressed out one time, and I simply said, "You can't add an hour to your life by worrying, so why worry?" The person I was speaking to responded, "Wow, that's so true." Right then, I was able to give God credit, "Not my words; Jesus said it first." I remembered Matthew 6:27 and used that as a way to plant the seed. People are naturally curious about God, and the string of questions that followed turned into a really fulfilling conversation. It was that simple. Finding scriptures that can be shared with non-believers is one way to introduce them to the wisdom of our God and the wonderful promises He makes to His children. You may not have to look far for an opportunity to speak God's Word; a lot of the time, God will bring them right to you. The best thing you can do is be prepared to act in kindness and speak God's Word.[76] In short, imitate Christ. Allow Jesus to live out His life in and through you.

# Afterword

I pray that this book has been a blessing to you. It has been a challenge to write, but I know that it will bless someone. My hope is that for you, the student reader, to be better equipped in the classroom, to have your faith strengthened, and some of those lingering questions answered. For the teachers in the faith, you have a responsibility to be a believer first. The students who are entrusted to you are no mistake. Be an ambassador of the kingdom first and foremost, and remember the importance of your student's eternity. Professors in the faith are tasked with much difficulty as well. Hold fast to Him whom you have believed and persevere. Parents of students, please inquire more deeply about what your children are learning. Students have a right to free and quality education. You have a right to know what they are being taught. I do not condone cancel culture, but I do believe parents need to have a more active role in discussing the content of what their children are being taught with their children. I have been tasked with writing this book and know that God's Word will not return to Him void. I would love to know how this book has blessed you. I continually pray for the education system and the impressionable minds that are entrusted to it. Go forth in love, peace, boldness, and perseverance to preach the message of the gospel. Thank you for your support, and may God bless you.

# Endnotes

[1] "He has made everything beautiful in its time. Also He has put eternity in their hearts, except that no one can find out the work that God does from beginning to end" (Ecclesiastes 3:11, NKJV).

[2] "And you will seek Me and find Me, when you search for Me with all your heart" (Jeremiah 29:13, NKJV).

[3] "The heart is deceitful above all things, And desperately wicked; Who can know it?" (Jeremiah 17:9, NKJV).

[4] "I, the Lord, search the heart, I test the mind, Even to give every man according to his ways, According to the fruit of his doings" (Jeremiah 17:10, NKJV).

[5] "So Jesus said to them, 'Because of your unbelief; for assuredly, I say to you, if you have faith as a mustard seed, you will say to this mountain, 'Move from here to there,' and it will move; and nothing will be impossible for you" (Matthew 17:20, NKJV).

[6] "For in it the righteousness of God is revealed from faith to faith; as it is written, 'The just shall live by faith'" (Romans 1:17, NKJV).
"But without faith it is impossible to please Him, for he who comes to God must believe ...that He is a rewarder of those who diligently seek Him" (Hebrews 11:6, NKJV).

[7] "Therefore take up the whole armor of God, that you may be able to withstand in the evil day, and having done all, to stand. Stand therefore, having girded your waist with truth, having put on the breastplate of righteousness, and having shod your feet with the preparation of the gospel of peace; above all, taking the shield of faith with which you will be able to quench all the fiery darts of the wicked one. And take the helmet of salvation, and the sword of the Spirit, which is the word of God" (Ephesians 6:13–17, NKJV).

[8] Richards, Olly. "World Exclusive: The Joker Speaks." Empire. Empire, November 28, 2007. https://www.empireonline.com/movies/news/world-exclusive-joker-speaks/.

[9] "And of every living thing of all flesh you shall bring two of every sort into the ark, to keep them alive with you; they shall be male and female" (Genesis 6:19, NKJV).

[10] "Do not lay up for yourselves treasures on earth, where moth and rust destroy and where thieves break in and steal; but lay up for yourselves treasures in heaven, where neither moth nor rust destroys and where thieves do not break in and steal" (Matthew 6:19–20, NKJV).

[11] "Behold, He who keeps Israel Shall neither slumber nor sleep" (Psalm 121:4, NKJV).

227

[12] "But God has chosen the foolish things of the world to put to shame the wise, and God has chosen the weak things of the world to put to shame the things which are mighty" (1 Corinthians 1:27, NKJV).

[13] "For the wisdom of the world is foolishness with God. For it is written, 'He catches the wise in their own craftiness'" (1 Corinthians 3:19, NKJV).

[14] "Beware lest anyone cheat you through philosophy and empty deceit, according to the tradition of men, according to the basic principles of the world, and not according to Christ" (Colossians 2:8, NKJV).

[15] "Not everyone who says to Me, 'Lord, Lord,' shall enter the kingdom of heaven, but he who does the will of My Father in heaven. Many will say to Me in that day, 'Lord, Lord, have we not prophesied in Your name, cast out demons in Your name, and done many wonders in Your name?' And then I will declare to them, 'I never knew you; depart from Me, you who practice lawlessness!'" (Matthew 7:21–23, NKJV).

[16] "You have heard that it was said, 'You shall love your neighbor and hate your enemy.' But I say to you, love your enemies, bless those who curse you, do good to those who hate you, and pray for those who spitefully use you and persecute you" (Matthew 5:43–44, NKJV).

[17] "But Jesus said to him, 'Put your sword in its place, for all who take the sword will perish by the sword'" (Matthew 26:52, NKJV).

[18] See Daniel chapter 2.

[19] "And God will wipe away every tear from their eyes; there shall be no more death, nor sorrow, nor crying. There shall be no more pain, for the former things have passed away" (Revelation 21:4, NKJV).

[20] "However, when He, the Spirit of truth, has come, He will guide you into all truth; for He will not speak on His own authority, but whatever He hears He will speak; and He will tell you things to come" (John 16:13, NKJV).

[21] "At that time Jesus answered and said, 'I thank You, Father, Lord of heaven and earth, that You have hidden these things from the wise and prudent and have revealed them to babes'" (Matthew 11:25, NKJV).

[22] "Bearing with one another, and forgiving one another, if anyone has a complaint against another; even as Christ forgave you, so you also must do" (Colossians 3:13, NKJV).

[23] "And just as you want men to do to you, you also do to them likewise" (Luke 6:31, NKJV).

[24] "'And you shall love the Lord your God with all your heart, with all your soul, with all your mind, and with all your strength.' This is the first commandment. And the second, like it, is this: 'You shall love your neighbor as yourself.' There is no other commandment greater than these" (Mark 12:30–31, NKJV).

[25] "I have not come to call the righteous, but sinners, to repentance" (Luke 5:32, NKJV).

[26] "And I urge you also, true companion, help these women who labored with me in the gospel, with Clement also, and the rest of my fellow workers, whose names are in the Book of Life" (Philippians 4:3, NKJV).

[27] "Let nothing be done through strife or vainglory; but in lowliness of mind let each esteem other better than themselves. Look not every man on his own things, but every man also on the things of others. Let this mind be in you, which was also in Christ Jesus" (Philippians 2:3–5, KJV).

[28] "'There was a certain creditor who had two debtors. One owed five hundred denarii, and the other fifty. And when they had nothing with which to repay, he freely forgave them both. Tell Me, therefore, which of them will love him more?' Simon answered and said, 'I suppose the one whom he forgave more.' And He said to him, 'You have rightly judged'" (Luke 7:41–43, NKJV).

[29] "There is no fear in love; but perfect love casts out fear, because fear involves torment. But he who fears has not been made perfect in love" (1 John 4:18, NKJV).

[30] "Inasmuch then as the children have partaken of flesh and blood, He Himself likewise shared in the same, that through death He might destroy him who had the power of death, that is, the devil, and release those who through fear of death were all their lifetime subject to bondage" (Hebrews 2:14–15, NKJV).

[31] "The heart is deceitful above all things, And desperately wicked; Who can know it?" (Jeremiah 17:9, NKJV).

[32] "And the Lord God commanded the man, saying, "Of every tree of the garden you may freely eat; but of the tree of the knowledge of good and evil you shall not eat, for in the day that you eat of it you shall surely die" (Genesis 2:16–17, NKJV).

[33] "Now the works of the flesh are evident, which are: adultery, fornication, uncleanness, lewdness, idolatry, sorcery, hatred, contentions, jealousies, outbursts of wrath, selfish ambitions, dissensions, heresies, envy, murders, drunkenness, revelries, and the like; of which I tell you beforehand, just as I also told you in time past, that those who practice such things will not inherit the kingdom of God" (Galatians 5:19–21, NKJV).

[34] "So when the woman saw that the tree was good for food, that it was pleasant to the eyes, and a tree desirable to make one wise, she took of its fruit and ate" (Genesis 3:6, NKJV).

[35] "For there is nothing hid, which shall not be manifested; neither was any thing kept secret, but that it should come abroad" (Mark 4:22, KJV).

[36] "But the fruit of the Spirit is love, joy, peace, longsuffering, kindness, good-

ness, faithfulness, gentleness, self-control. Against such there is no law" (Galatians 5:22–23, NKJV).

[37] "If your hand causes you to sin, cut it off. It is better for you to enter into life maimed, rather than having two hands, to go to hell, into the fire that shall never be quenched— where 'Their worm does not die And the fire is not quenched'" (Mark 9:43–44, NKJV).

[38] "So then every one of us shall give account of himself to God" (Romans 14:12, KJV).

[39] "But this is the covenant that I will make with the house of Israel after those days, says the Lord: I will put My law in their minds, and write in on their hearts; and I will be their God, and they shall be My people" (Jeremiah 31:33, NKJV).

[40] "A good man out of the good treasure of his heart brings forth good; and an evil man out of the evil treasure of his heart brings forth evil. For out of the abundance of the heart his mouth speaks" (Luke 6:45, NKJV).

[41] "When His disciples heard it, they were greatly astonished, saying, 'Who then can be saved?' But Jesus looked at them and said to them, 'With men this is impossible, but with God all things are possible'" (Matthew 19:25–26, NKJV).

[42] "I am the good shepherd. The good shepherd gives His life for the sheep" (John 10:11, NKJV).

[43] "For 'whoever calls on the name of the Lord shall be saved'" (Romans 10:13, NKJV).

[44] "But the very hairs of your head are all numbered. Do not fear therefore; you are of more value than many sparrows" (Luke 12:7, NKJV).

[45] "Call to Me, and I will answer you, and show you great and mighty things, which you do not know" (Jeremiah 33:3, NKJV).

[46] "For you did not receive the spirit of bondage again to fear, but you received the Spirit of adoption by whom we cry out, 'Abba, Father'" (Romans 8:15, NKJV).

[47] "For all have sinned and fall short of the glory God" (Romans 3:23, NKJV).

[48] "Instead he is patient with you, not wanting anyone to perish, but everyone to come to repentance" (2 Peter 3:9, NIV).

[49] "The wages of sin is death; but the gift of God is eternal life through Jesus Christ our Lord" (Romans 6:23, KJV).

[50] "Do not be deceived, God is not mocked; for whatever a man sows, that he will also reap" (Galatians 6:7, NKJV).

[51] "For we must all appear before the judgment seat of Christ; that every one may receive the things done in his body, according to that he hath done, whether

it be good or bad" (2 Corinthians 5:10, KJV).

[52] "By this all will know that you are My disciples, if you have love for one another" (John 13:35, NKJV).

[53] "There is no fear in love; but perfect love casts our fear, because fear involves torment. But he who fear has not been made perfect in love" (1 John 4:18, NKJV).

[54] "Greater love has no one than this, than to lay down one's life for his friends" (John 15:13, NKJV).

[55] "No longer do I call you servants, for a servant does not know what his master is doing; but I have called you friends, for all things that I heard from My Father I have made known to you. You did not choose Me, but I chose you and appointed you that you should go and bear fruit, and that your fruit should remain, that whatever you ask the Father in My name He may give you. These things I command you, that you love one another" (John 15:15–17, NKJV).

[56] "Now may the God of hope fill you with all joy and peace in believing, that you may abound in hope by the power of the Holy Spirit" (Romans 15:13, NKJV).

[57] "Through the Lord's mercies we are not consumed, Because His compassions fail not. They are new every morning; Great is Your faithfulness" (Lamentations 3:22–23, NKJV).

[58] "Therefore, having these promises, beloved, let us cleanse ourselves from all filthiness of the flesh and spirit, perfecting holiness in the fear of God" (2 Corinthians 7:1, NKJV).

[59] "No temptation has overtaken you except such as is common to man; but God is faithful, who will not allow you to be tempted beyond what you are able, but with the temptation will also make the way of escape, that you may be able to bear it" (1 Corinthians 10:13, NKJV).

[60] "Can a woman forget her nursing child, And not have compassion on the son of her womb? Surely they may forget, Yet I will not forget you. See, I have inscribed you on the palms of My hands; Your walls are continually before Me" (Isaiah 49:15–16, NKJV).

[61] "The steps of a good man are ordered by the Lord, And He delights in his way" (Psalm 37:23, NKJV).

[62] "For by grace you have been saved through faith, and that not of yourselves; it is the gift of God" (Ephesians 2:8, NKJV).

[63] "For whom He foreknew, He also predestined to be conformed to the image of His Son, that He might be the firstborn among many brethren" (Romans 8:29, NKJV).

[64] "When a man's ways please the Lord, He makes even his enemies to be at

peace with him" (Proverbs 16:7, NKJV).

[65] "The message of the cross is foolishness to those who are perishing, but to us who are being saved it is the power of God" (1 Corinthians 1:18, NKJV).

[66] "Enter by the narrow gate; for wide is the gate and broad is the way that leads to destruction, and there are many who go in by it. Because narrow is the gate and difficult is the way which leads to life, and there are few who find it" (Matthew 7:13–14, NKJV).

[67] "Let your speech always be with grace, seasoned with salt, that you may know how you ought to answer each one" (Colossians 4:6, NKJV).

[68] "By this all will know that you are My disciples, if you have love for one another" (John 13:35, NKJV).

[69] "Thus also faith by itself, if it does not have works, is dead. But someone will say, 'You have faith, and I have works.' Show me your faith without your works, and I will show you my faith by my works" (James 2:17–18, NKJV).

[70] "And being found in appearance as a man, He humbled Himself and became obedient to the point of death, even the death of the cross" (Philippians 2:8, NKJV).

[71] "But seek first the kingdom of God and His righteousness, and all these things shall be added to you" (Matthew 6:33, NKJV).

[72] "Delight yourself also in the Lord, And He shall give you the desires of your heart" (Psalm 37:4, NKJV).

[73] "These things I have spoken to you, that in Me you may have peace. In the world you will have tribulation; but be of good cheer, I have overcome the world" (John 16:33, NKJV).

[74] "And God will wipe away every tear from their eyes; there shall be no more death, nor sorrow, nor crying. There shall be no more pain, for the former things have passed away" (Revelation 21:4, NKJV).

[75] "Now faith is the substance of things hoped for, the evidence of things not seen" (Hebrews 11:1, NKJV).

[76] "But sanctify the Lord God in your hearts, and always be ready to give a defense to everyone who asks you a reason for the hope that is in you" (1 Peter 3:15, NKJV).

CPSIA information can be obtained
at www.ICGtesting.com
Printed in the USA
LVHW021841261122
733860LV00007B/308